Pairpoint Lamp Catalog

Pairpoint Lamp Catalog

Shade Shapes Papillon through Windsor & Related Materials

Old Dartmouth Historical Society
New Bedford Whaling Museum

Foreword by Louis O. St. Aubin, Jr.

Schiffer Publishing Ltd

4880 Lower Valley Road, Atglen, PA 19310 USA

The Pairpoint Lamp Catalog continues with Plates #1 through #288 in another volume, *Pairpoint Lamp Catalog, Shade Shapes **Ambero** through **Panel***.

Acknowledgment is gratefully extended to Louis O. St. Aubin, Jr. for guiding this book and identifying the shade decorations; Judith M. Downey, Librarian of the New Bedford Whaling Museum, for shepherding and indexing the book and assisting with caption information; Mary Jean Blasdale, Collections Manager of the museum; and Candace Heald, Director of Programs of the museum; and Bruce M. Waters, photographer. Special thanks goes to Helen E. Frasier, who donated the catalog, and to the generous donors who have enriched the holdings of glass and glass related collections of the New Bedford Whaling Museum.

Library of Congress Cataloging-in-Publication Data

Pairpoint lamp catalog: shade shapes Papillon through Windsor & related material/The Pairpoint Corporation.
    p. cm.
    ISBN 0-7643-1335-5
    1. Pairpoint Glass Works--Catalogs. 2. Painted lampshades--Massachusetts--New Bedford--Catalogs. I. Pairpoint Glass Works.
    NK5436.P35 A4 2001
    749'.63--dc21
                                    00-013144

Copyright © 2001 by Old Dartmouth Historical Society

All rights reserved. No part of this work may be reproduced or used in any form or by any means—graphic, electronic, or mechanical, including photocopying or information storage and retrieval systems—without written permission from the copyright holder.
"Schiffer," "Schiffer Publishing Ltd. & Design," and the "Design of pen and inkwell" are registered trademarks of Schiffer Publishing Ltd.

Designed by "Sue"
Type set in Zaph Chancery Bd BT/Aldine 721

ISBN: 0-7643-1335-5
Printed in China

Published by Schiffer Publishing Ltd.
4880 Lower Valley Road
Atglen, PA 19310
Phone: (610) 593-1777; Fax: (610) 593-2002
E-mail: Schifferbk@aol.com
Please visit our web site catalog at **www.schifferbooks.com**
We are always looking for people to write books on new and related subjects. If you have an idea for a book, please contact us at the above address.

This book may be purchased from the publisher.
Include $3.95 for shipping. Please try your bookstore first.
You may write for a free catalog.

In Europe, Schiffer books are distributed by
Bushwood Books
6 Marksbury Ave. Kew Gardens
Surrey TW9 4JF England
Phone: 44 (0)20 8392-8585; Fax: 44 (0)20 8392-9876
E-mail: Bushwd@aol.com
Free postage in the UK. Europe: air mail at cost.
Please try your bookstore first.

Contents

Foreword 6

Chrononlogy of Glass Manufacturing in
    New Bedford, Massachusetts 7

Years of Production for Bases, Finishes,
    and Materials of Pairpoint Lamps 7

The Catalog, Plates 289-514 arranged
    alphabetically by shade shapes 8

Related Materials
    Electric Candles with Parchment Shades, Plates 515-524
    Color Printed Pages, Plates 525-572

Index 287

Foreword

Three remarkable women contributed to preserving this catalog. It was rescued from the Pairpoint factory about 1940 by Eleanor H. Bowman, a Pairpoint employee who found the catalogue in a factory showroom. Mr. Gundersen, manager and namesake of the Gundersen Glass Works, gave the catalog to her and said it was the original factory showroom catalogue that was in use for thirty years. A relative of Miss Bowman's later sold the catalog to antiques dealer Sadie Lowe, which made Miss Bowman furious. Still later, Mrs. Lowe sold the catalog to pioneering collector Helen E. Frasier, who realized its importance as the most complete and authentic record of the lamps known to exist. Mrs. Frasier admired and protected this remarkable work until 1988, when she donated it to the New Bedford Whaling Museum in New Bedford, Massachusetts, where it is preserved. Now it is being published so that a wider audience can see and appreciate the lamps of The Pairpoint Corporation.

Word has just arrived that a Pairpoint Lilac Puffy table lamp has been sold for in excess of $145,000. Also, a large Begonia leaf brought over $67,000 and an Orange Tree sold for over $64,000. This is quite a change from 1974, when the first book devoted solely to the lamps produced by the Pairpoint Corporation, my *Pairpoint Lamps: A Collector's Guide,* was published.

In 1968, I organized the first public exhibit of Pairpoint lamps as part of the New Bedford Antiques Show. Over thirty lamps were on display, including many Puffy lamps. It was the first public exhibit to bring attention to the artistic merit of these lamps. This antiques show, managed by my mother and late father, and the exhibit marked the beginning of my intense interest in the lamps.

Nearly thirty years later, I curated a major exhibit at the New Bedford Whaling Museum which featured an outstanding display of the rarest types of Pairpoint lamps. This and Sheila and Edward Malakoff's book about them have contributed to the present appreciation and demand for Pairpoint lamps.

Louis O. St. Aubin, Jr.
October, 2000

Chronology of Glass Manufacturing in New Bedford, Massachusetts

1867 New Bedford Glass Works opened in New Bedford, located on the waterfront of the Acushnet River

1870 Mt. Washington Glass Works moved from Boston to occupy the recently closed factory of the New Bedford Glass Works

1871 Alfred and Harry Smith came to New Bedford to establish the decorating shop at Mt. Washington

1876 Mt. Washington Glass Works reorganized into Mt. Washington Glass Company
Both Mt. Washington and Smith Brothers exhibited separately at the Centennial Exposition at Philadelphia and both won awards

1880 Pairpoint Manufacturing Company established manufacturing silver plate items. Company located adjacent to Mt Washington on the waterfront

1894 Mt. Washington Glass Company and Pairpoint Manufacturing Co. merged

1900 Pairpoint Manufacturing Co. reorganized into the Pairpoint Corporation

1907 Pairpoint applied for and received patent for "electrolier" lamps

1938 Pairpoint Corp. closed glass and silver departments; company became known as National Pairpoint Co.

1939 Gundersen Glass Works, Inc. established and continued production of glass in Pairpoint plant

1940 Corcoran Fine Arts, Inc. established and continued silver plate production in Pairpoint plant; proved to be short lived effort as closed in 1941

1952 Gundersen Glass Works was bought out by National Pairpoint Company and became Gundersen-Pairpoint Glass Works

1957 Gundersen-Pairpoint Glass Works closed and company left New Bedford

1970 A glass company was established by Tobert Bryden as Pairpoint Glass Company in Sagamore, Massachusetts

Years of Production for Bases, Finishes, and Materials of Pairpoint Lamps

1900s	Japanese Bronze		Copper, Gray
1910	Old Brass Green		French Gray - plain and engraved
	(green paint in engraving)	1920s	Old Brass
	Antique or Gun Metal		Egyptian Brass
	(Antique = green verdi finish)		Flemish
	Old Brass		Antique Bronze
1910-1914	Glass Inserts		Butler Silver
1910-1915	Matching All Glass Base	1926	Cut Glass Columns for Floor Lamps
1915	Bronze	1930s	Butler Silver
	Mahogany with Brass Trim		Egyptian Brass
	Silver Plain or Engraved		Flemish
	French Gray		Old Brass
	New Antique Finish		

The Catalog

Caption Notes
The Pairpoint Lamp Catalog continues with Plates #1 through #288 in another volume, *Pairpoint Lamp Catalog, Shade Shapes **Ambero** through **Panel***.

Plate captions include the following elements:
1. **shade shape**, as listed on the catalog sheets
2. shade's **decoration name**; if it appears in *italics*- then the name has been assigned by Louis O. St. Aubin, Jr.; if it appears in plain type- then the name has been taken from the catalog sheets
3. shade's **decoration number**
4. **base number**, as taken from the catalog sheets
5. **dates of production** assigned, based on the locations of the showrooms indicated on the catalog sheets

OLD BRASS, EGYPTIAN BRASS, ANTIQUE AND FLEMISH FINISH.

Base, C3066. 2-light,	$10.45	Butler Silver,	$13.20
No. 320-14′ Papillon shade,	9.75	Shade,	9.75
	$20.20		$22.95

Height overall, 23½ inches

THE PAIRPOINT CORPORATION
NEW BEDFORD, MASS.
43-47 West 23rd Street. - New York City
150 Post Street, Room 300, San Francisco, Cal.
Neg. 785

Plate 289. Papillon shade. Puffy. *Pastel Papillon with wild rose* decoration #320. Base #C3066. 1931-1935.

No. B 3044.   ELECTROLIER, with 8 Feet Silk Cord, Height of Body, 7½ inches.

THE PAIRPOINT CORPORATION,
NEW BEDFORD, MASS.
38 Murray Street, New York City.
485 St. Catherine St., Montreal, Canada.
717 Market St., San Francisco, Cal.
NEG. 858 A

Less Shade, Copper, Gray Finish, $7.50

No. 931. 8 inch Papillion Shade, $7.00

TRADE MARK

Plate 290. Papillon shade. Puffy. *Papillon with roses and rare green background* decoration #931 (close top). Base #B3044. 1907-1910.

No. B 3048.   ELECTROLIER, with 8 Feet Silk Cord, Height of Body, 6½ inches.

THE PAIRPOINT CORPORATION,
NEW BEDFORD, MASS.
38 Murray Street, New York City.
485 St. Catherine St., Montreal, Canada.
717 Market St., San Francisco, Cal.
Neg. 657 A

Less Shade, Old Brass, $6.50
No. 930. 8 inch Papillion Shade, $7.00

Plate 291. Papillon shade. Puffy. *Papillon on white and green mottled background* decoration #930 (close top). Base #B3048. 1907-1910.

No. B 3012. ELECTROLIER, with 8 Feet Silk Cord, Height of Body, 16 inches.

THE PAIRPOINT CORPORATION.
NEW BEDFORD, MASS.
38 Murray Street, New York City.
36 St. Antoine St., Montreal, Canada.
717 Market St., San Francisco, Cal.
NEG. 477 A

Less Shade, Old Brass, Plain, $14.50
" " " Engraved, 16.00
Two Lights, $4.00 extra.
No. 930. 14 inch Papillion Shade, $15.00

Plate 292. Papillon shade . Puffy. *Papillon with red roses on white and green mottled background* decoration #931 (close top). Base #B3012. 1907.

No. C3066. ELECTROLIER, with 8 Feet Silk Cord, Height of Body, 13 inches.

(Complete Height to Top of Shade, 23½ inches)
Base, Old Brass, Flemish Brass, Butler or New Antique Finish, Two Light,
No. 930. 14 inch Papillon Shade, Complete,

THE PAIRPOINT CORPORATION
NEW BEDFORD, MASS.
43-47 West 28rd. Street. New York City
150 Post Street. Room 800. San Francisco, Cal.
228 Coristine Building, St. Nicholas Street
Montreal, Canada.
Neg. 1014

24.60
28.10
52.70

TRADE MARK

Plate 293. Papillon shade. Puffy. *Papillon with roses* decoration #930. Base #C3066. 1930.

No. 3047½. ELECTROLIER. With 7 Feet Silk Cord, Height to Top of Shade, 14½ inches.

THE PAIRPOINT CORPORATION,
NEW BEDFORD, MASS.
43-47 West 23rd St., New York City.
402 Columbus Memorial Bldg., Chicago.
140 Geary St., San Francisco, Cal.
Coristine Building, St. Nicholas St.,
NEG. 585   Montreal, Canada.

Base, One Light, Height, 8½ inches, Plain Old Brass, Antique or Bronze, $7.30
(Fitted with Push Button Socket.)
No. 895. 8 inch Papillon Shade,   5.95

Complete, $13.25

TRADE

Plate 294. Papillon shade. Puffy. *Papillon with roses on white and pink mottled background* decoration #895. Base #3047 1/2. 1915.

Plate 295. Paris shade. *Napoli style oriental Poppy* decoration #931. Base #3039. 1900-1903.

No. B 3000. ELECTROLIER. With 8 Feet Silk Cord, Height of Body, 15 inches.

THE PAIRPOINT CORPORATION,
NEW BEDFORD, MASS.
38 Murray Street, New York City.
Coristine Building, St. Nicholas St.,
Montreal, Canada.
717 Market St., San Francisco, Cal.
NEG 82

One Light, Less Shade, Old Brass Green, Antique or Gun Metal, $15.00
Two Light, $19.00
No. 830. 18 inch Pisa Shade, $24.00

Plate 296. Pisa shade. Ribbed. *Roses and scrolls* decoration #830. Base #B3000. 1911-1914.

No. B 3065. ELECTROLIER. With 8 Feet Silk Cord, Height of Body, 16 inches.

One Light, Less Shade, Plain, Old Brass, Antique Green, or Gun Metal $18.00 Two Light, $22.00
" " Engraved, " Green and Red " " 19.00 " 23.00

No. 1700. 18 inch Pisa Shade, $26.00

THE PAIRPOINT CORPORATION,
NEW BEDFORD, MASS.
38 Murray Street, New York City.
Coristine Building, St. Nicholas St.,
Montreal, Canada.
717 Market St., San Francisco, Cal.
NEG 83

TRADE

Plate 297. Pisa shade. Ribbed. *Lilac and lattice* decoration #1700. Base #B3065. 1911-1914.

Plate 298. Pisa shade. Ribbed. *Egyptian merchant* decoration #1710. Base #C3005 (glass column insert). No date.

No. C 3061. ELECTROLIER, with 8 Feet Silk Cord. Height of Body, 10 inches.
Plain, One Light, Less Shade, Old Brass, Antique or Gun Metal, $8.20

THE PAIRPOINT CORPORATION,
NEW BEDFORD, MASS.
38 Murray Street, New York City.
Coristine Building, St. Nicholas St.,
Montreal, Canada.
717 Market St., San Francisco, Cal.
NEG. 366

No. 509. 12 inch Plymouth Shade, $6.40

TRADE P MA

Plate 299. Plymouth shade. *Woman on path and landscape* decoration #509. Base #C3061. 1911-1914.

No. C 3061   ELECTROLIER, with 8 Feet Silk Cord, Height of Body, 10 inches.
Special Two Light Fixture, Less Shade, Old Brass, Antique or Gun Metal, $8.20

THE PAIRPOINT CORPORATION,
NEW BEDFORD, MASS.
38 Murray Street, New York City.
Coristine Building, St. Nicholas St.,
Montreal, Canada.
717 Market St., San Francisco, Cal.
Neg. 457

No. 659. 12 inch Plymouth Shade, $6.80

TRADE

Plate 300. Plymouth shade. *Azalea and scrolls* decoration #659. Base #C3061. 1911-1914.

No. C 3060.   ELECTROLIER, with 8 Feet Silk Cord, Height of Body, 9½ inches.
Special Two Light Fixture, Less Shade, Old Brass Green, Antique or Gun Metal, $7.75

THE PAIRPOINT CORPORATION,
NEW BEDFORD, MASS.
38 Murray Street, New York City.
Coristine Building, St. Nicholas St.,
Montreal, Canada.
717 Market St., San Francisco, Cal.
N EG. 447

No. 660.   12 inch Plymouth Shade, $9.10

TRADE

Plate 301. Plymouth shade. *Yellow rose* decoration #660. Base #C3060. 1911-1914.

No. B 3067. ELECTROLIER, with 8 Feet Silk Cord, Height of Body, 12 inches.
Special Two Light Fixture, Less Shade, Old Brass, Gun Metal or Antique, $10.00
"   "   "   "   Engraved Old Brass Green or Gun Metal,   12.00
Fancy Coloring, $1.50 Extra.
No. 661.   12 inch Plymouth Shade, $10.00

THE PAIRPOINT CORPORATION,
NEW BEDFORD, MASS.
38 Murray Street, New York City.
Coristine Building, St. Nicholas St.,
Montreal, Canada.
717 Market St., San Francisco, Cal.
NEG. 452

TRADE

Plate 302. Plymouth shade. *Lyre wreath and florals* decoration #661. Base #B3067. 1911-1914.

No. C 3067 748. ELECTROLIER. With 8 Feet Silk Cord, Height of Body, 12½ inches. Complete, $19.
Lamp Base, Less Shade, with Special Two Light Fixture, Old Brass Fittings, $12.30
No. 748. 12 inch Plymouth Shade, $7.30

THE PAIRPOINT CORPORATION,
NEW BEDFORD, MASS.
38 Murray Street, New York City.
Coristine Building, St. Nicholas St.,
Montreal, Canada.
717 Market St., San Francisco, Cal.
NEG. 566

TRADE P MARK

Plate 303. Plymouth shade. *Wisteria* decoration #748. Base #C3067/748 (matching glass base). 1911-1914.

No. C 3060. ELECTROLIER, with 8 Feet Silk Cord. Height of Body, 10 inches.
Plain, One Light, Less Shade, Old Brass Green, Antique or Gun Metal, $7.75

THE PAIRPOINT CORPORATION.
NEW BEDFORD, MASS.
38 Murray Street, New York City.
Coristine Building, St. Nicholas St.,
Montreal, Canada.
717 Market St., San Francisco, Cal.
Neg. 365

No. 810. 12 inch Plymouth Shade, $6.40

TRADE MA

Plate 304. Plymouth shade. *Hollyhocks* decoration #810. Base #C3060. 1911-1914.

No. B 3041.   ELECTROLIER, with 8 Feet Silk Cord, Height of Body, 13½ inches.

THE PAIRPOINT CORPORATION,
NEW BEDFORD, MASS.
38 Murray Street, New York City.
485 St. Catherine St., Montreal, Canada.
717 Market St., San Francisco, Cal.
Neg. 670 A

One Light, Less Shade, Copper, Gray Finish, $14.50
Two   "   "   "   "   "   18.50
No. 986.   12 inch Plymouth Shade, $7.00

TRADE MARK

Plate 305. Plymouth shade. *Bearded iris* decoration #986. Base #B3041. 1907-1910.

No. B 3042.   ELECTROLIER, with 8 Feet Silk Cord, Height of Body, 13½ inches.

THE PAIRPOINT CORPORATION,
NEW BEDFORD, MASS.
38 Murray Street, New York City.
485 St. Catherine St., Montreal, Canada.
717 Market St., San Francisco, Cal.
Neg. 671 A

One Light, Less Shade, Copper, Gray Finish, $14.50
Two   "   "   "   "   "   18.50

No. 987. 12 inch Plymouth Shade, $9.00

Plate 306. Plymouth shade. *Scroll border with roses* decoration #987. Base #B3042. 1907-1910.

No. B 3011. ELECTROLIER, with 8 Feet Silk Cord, Height of Body, 15 inches.

THE PAIRPOINT CORPORATION,
NEW BEDFORD, MASS.
38 Murray Street, New York City.
485 St. Catherine St., Montreal, Canada.
717 Market St., San Francisco, Cal.
NEG. 582 A

Less Shade, Old Brass, Plain, $12.00
" " Engraved, 13.00
Double Light $4.00 extra.
No. 1359. 12 inch Plymouth Shade, 15.00

TRADE P MARK

Plate 307. Plymouth shade. *Flemish wisteria* decoration #1359. Base #B3011. 1907-1910.

No. B 3009.　ELECTROLIER, with 8 Feet Silk Cord, Height of Body, 11½ inches.

THE PAIRPOINT CORPORATION.
NEW BEDFORD, MASS.
38 Murray Street, New York City.
36 St. Antoine St., Montreal, Canada.
717 Market St., San Francisco, Cal.
Neg. 487 A.

Less Shade, Engraved, Old Brass,　$12.50
"　"　"　"　Two Lights,　16.50
No. 1368.　12 inch Plymouth Shade,　12.00

TRADE MARK

Plate 308. Plymouth shade. *Stylized leaves and tulips* decoration #1368. Base #B3009. 1907.

No. B 3000. ELECTROLIER, with 8 Feet Silk Cord, Height of Body, 15 inches.

THE PAIRPOINT CORPORATION.
NEW BEDFORD, MASS.
38 Murray Street, New York City.
36 St. Antoine St., Montreal, Canada.
717 Market St., San Francisco, Cal.
NEG. 479 A

Less Shade, Old Brass, $15.00
" " Two Lights, 19.00
No. 1369. 12 inch Plymouth Shade, $15.00

Plate 309. Plymouth shade. *Greek key with panels* decoration #1369. Base #B3000. 1907.

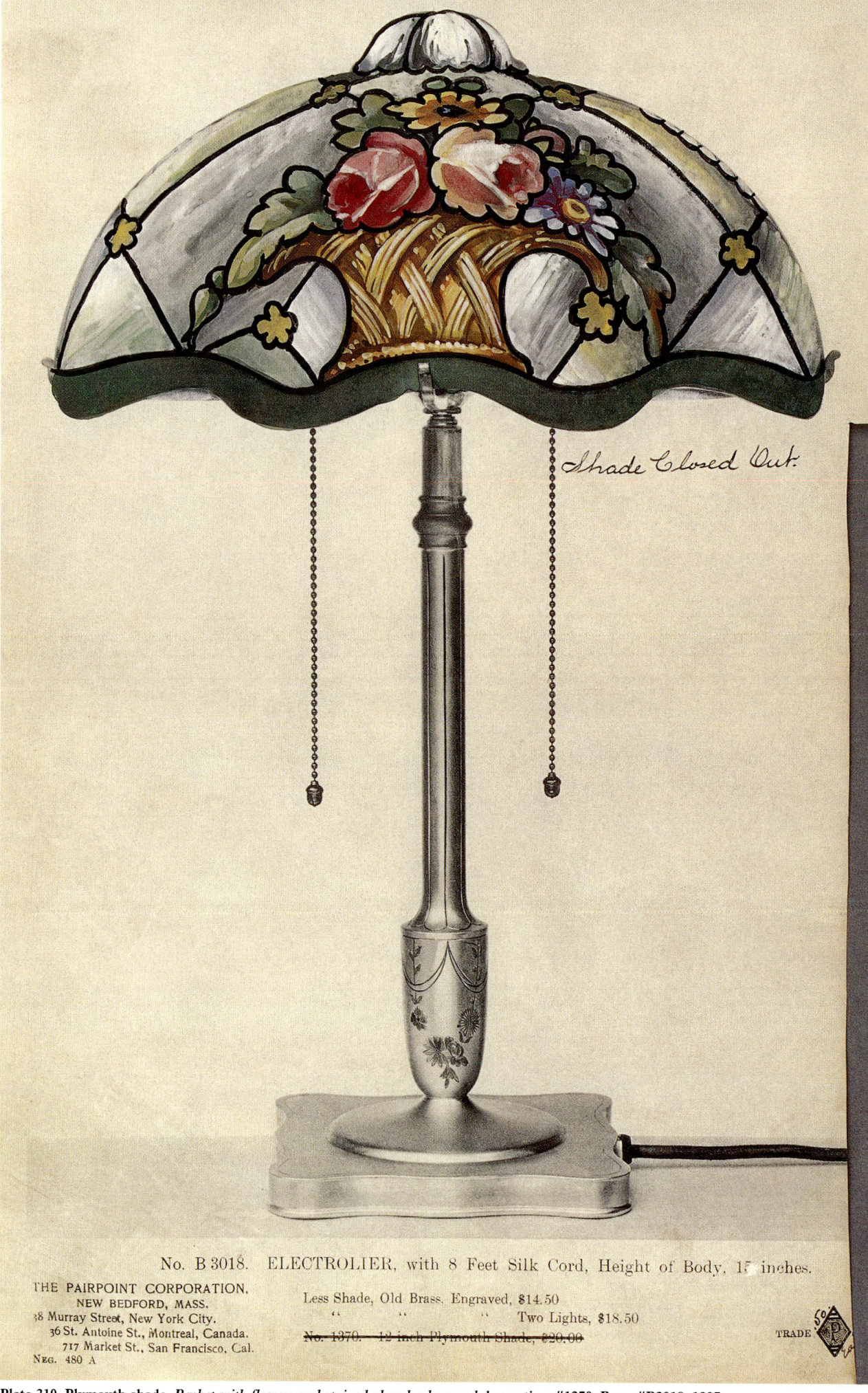

No. B 3018.   ELECTROLIER, with 8 Feet Silk Cord, Height of Body, 17 inches.

THE PAIRPOINT CORPORATION,
NEW BEDFORD, MASS.
38 Murray Street, New York City.
36 St. Antoine St., Montreal, Canada.
717 Market St., San Francisco, Cal.
NEG. 480 A

Less Shade, Old Brass. Engraved, $14.50
"   "   "   Two Lights, $18.50
No. 1370.   12 inch Plymouth Shade, $20.00

Shade Closed Out.

TRADE

Plate 310. Plymouth shade. *Basket with flowers and stained glass background decoration #1370. Base #B3018. 1907.*

No. B 3016.   ELECTROLIER, with 8 Feet Silk Cord, Height of Body, 13 inches.

THE PAIRPOINT CORPORATION,
NEW BEDFORD, MASS.
38 Murray Street, New York City.
36 St. Antoine St., Montreal, Canada.
717 Market St., San Francisco, Cal.
NEG. 485 A

Less Shade, Old Brass, $13.00
"   "   Two Lights, $17.00
No. 1371.   12 inch Plymouth Shade, $15.00

TRADE

Plate 311. Plymouth shade. *Flemish Parrot tulip* decoration #1371. Base #B3016. 1907.

No. 3036   ELECTROLIER, with 8 Feet Silk Cord, Height of Body, 13 inches.

THE PAIRPOINT CORPORATION.
NEW BEDFORD, MASS.
38 Murray Street, New York City.
36 St. Antoine St., Montreal, Canada.
717 Market St., San Francisco, Cal.
Neg. 532 A

Less Shade, Plain, Old Brass or Jap. Bronze, 11.00
" Engraved, " " " " 14.50
With Two Lights, $4.00 extra.
No. 1372.   12 inch Plymouth Shade, $15.00

Plate 312. Plymouth shade. *Flemish Grapes and vine* decoration #1372. Base #3036. 1907.

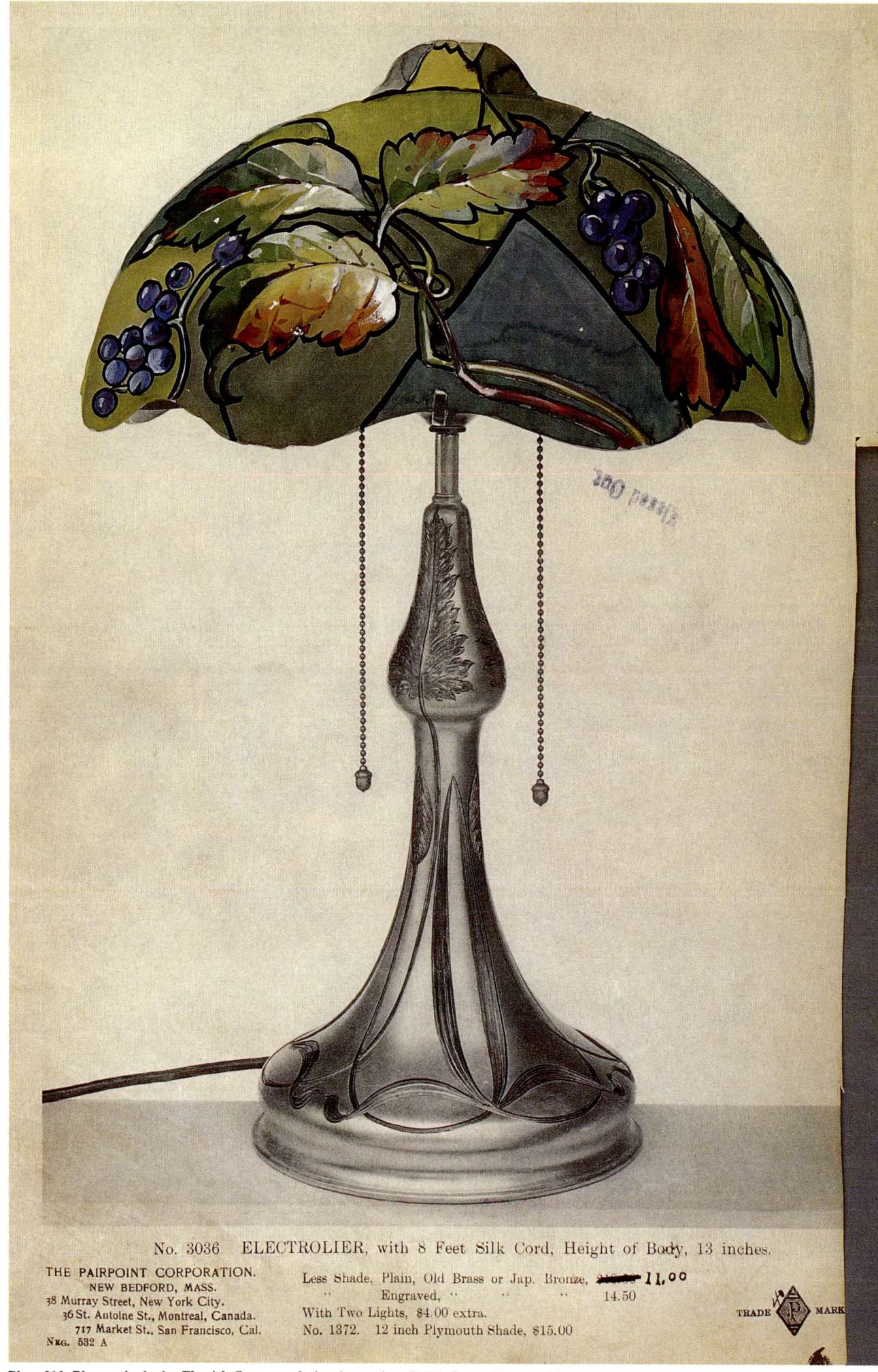

No. B 3010.   ELECTROLIER, with 8 Feet Silk Cord, Height of Body, 13 inches.

THE PAIRPOINT CORPORATION.
NEW BEDFORD, MASS.
38 Murray Street, New York City.
36 St. Antoine St., Montreal, Canada.
717 Market St., San Francisco, Cal.
NEG. 486 A

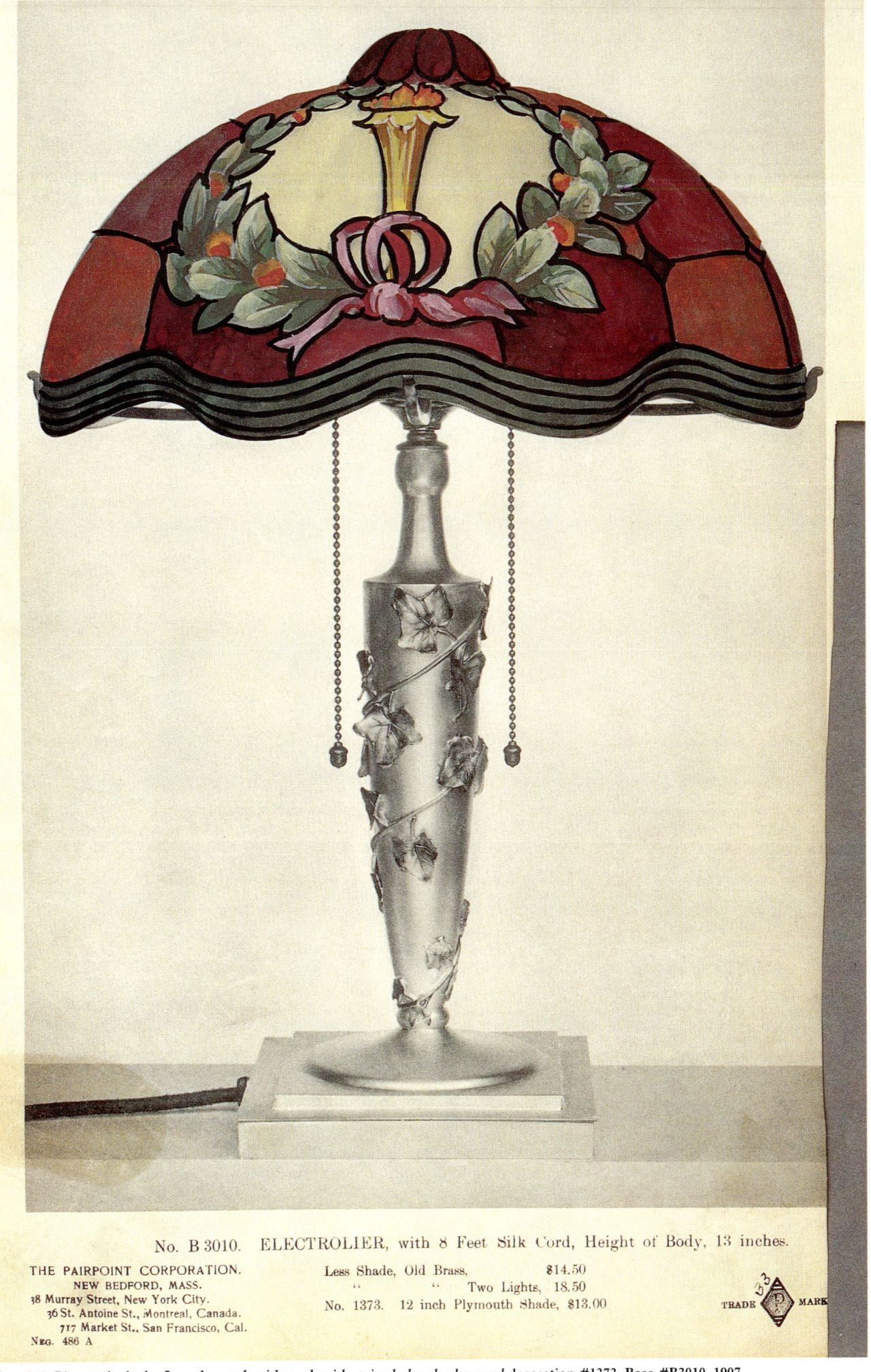

Less Shade, Old Brass, $14.50
"   "   Two Lights,   18.50
No. 1373.   12 inch Plymouth Shade, $13.00

Plate 313. Plymouth shade. *Laurel wreath with torch with stained glass background* decoration #1373. Base #B3010. 1907.

Shade Closed Out.

No. B 3008.   ELECTROLIER, with 8 Feet Silk Cord, Height of Body, 13½ inches.

THE PAIRPOINT CORPORATION,
NEW BEDFORD, MASS.
38 Murray Street, New York City.
36 St. Antoine St., Montreal, Canada.
717 Market St., San Francisco, Cal.
NEG. 481 A

Less Shade, Old Brass, Plain, $14.50
"   "   Eng.,   16.00
With Two Lights, $4.00 extra.
No. 1976. 12 inch Plymouth Shade, $20.00

TRADE

Plate 314. Plymouth shade. *Stained glass window* decoration #1376. Base #B3008. 1907.

No. B 3016.   ELECTROLIER, with 8 Feet Silk Cord, Height of Body, 13 inches.

THE PAIRPOINT CORPORATION,
NEW BEDFORD, MASS.
38 Murray Street, New York City.
485 St. Catherine St., Montreal, Canada.
717 Market St., San Francisco, Cal.
NEG. 583 A

Less Shade, Old Brass, $13.00
"   "   Double Light, 17.00
No. 1380. 12 inch Plymouth Shade, 13.00

TRADE MARK

Plate 315. Plymouth shade. *Wild Roses with white and green panels* decoration #1380. Base #B3016. 1907-1910.

No. B 3008. ELECTROLIER, with 8 Feet Silk Cord, Height of Body, 13¾ inches.

THE PAIRPOINT CORPORATION.
NEW BEDFORD, MASS.
38 Murray Street, New York City.
485 St. Catherine St., Montreal, Canada.
717 Market St., San Francisco, Cal.
NEG 726 A

With Two Lights, $4.00 extra.
No. 1385. 12 inch Plymouth Shade, $10.00

TRADE MARK

COPY

Plate 316. Plymouth shade. *Lily of the valley on red background* decoration #1385. Base #B3008. 1907-1910.

No. B 3028.   ELECTROLIER, with 8 Feet Silk Cord, Height of Body, 11 inches.

THE PAIRPOINT CORPORATION,
NEW BEDFORD, MASS.
38 Murray Street, New York City.
485 St. Catherine St., Montreal, Canada.
717 Market St., San Francisco, Cal.
Neg. 640 A

One Light, Less Shade, Copper, Metal Trimmings, $12.00
Two   "   "   "   "   "   16.00

No. 1552. 12 inch Plymouth Shade, $10.00

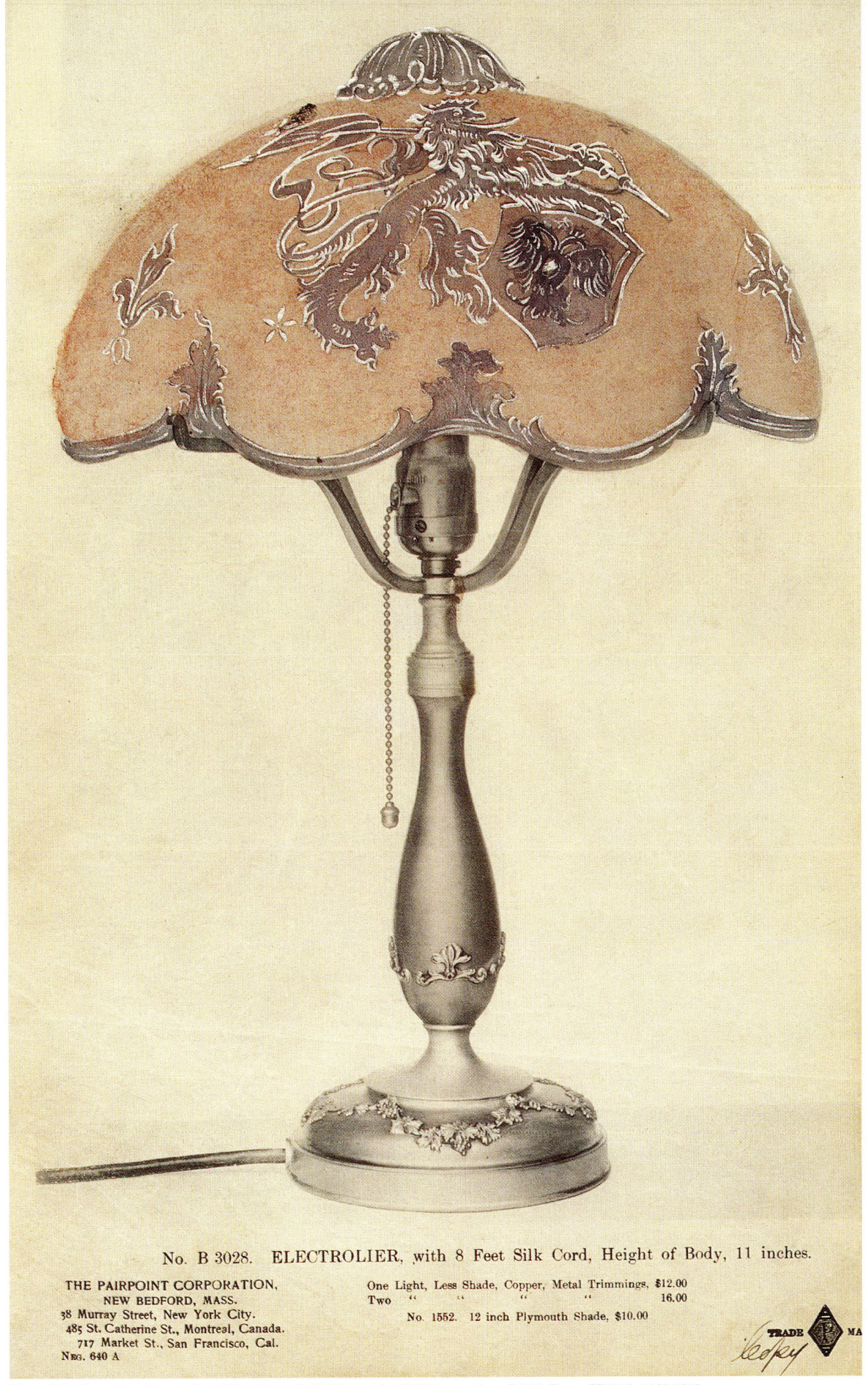

Plate 317. Plymouth shade. *Royal Flemish style Griffin with shield* decoration #1552. Base #B3028. 1907-1910.

No. D3009. ELECTROLIER. With 8 Feet Silk Cord, Height to Top of Shade, 20½ inches.

THE PAIRPOINT CORPORATION,
NEW BEDFORD, MASS.
43-47 West 23rd St., New York City.
402 Columbus Memorial Bldg., Chicago.
140 Geary St., San Francisco, Cal.
Coristine Building, St. Nicholas St.,
Montreal, Canada.
NEG. 623

Base, Solid Mahogany, Height. 11¾ inches, Two Light, $7.50
No. 882. 16 inch Pressed Red Poinsettia Shade. 13.65

Complete, $21.15

Plate 318. Poinsettia shade. Puffy. Pressed Red decoration #882. Base #D3009 (mahogany). 1915.

No. B 3041. **ELECTROLIER**, with 8 Feet Silk Cord. Height of Body, 13 inches.
One Light, Less Shade, Old Brass Green, Antique or Gun Metal, $14.50   Two Lights, $18.50

THE PAIRPOINT CORPORATION,
NEW BEDFORD, MASS.
38 Murray Street, New York City.
Coristine Building, St. Nicholas St.,
Montreal, Canada.
717 Market St., San Francisco, Cal.

No. 934   14 inch Pompey Shade, $10.00

NEG. 968 A

TRADE MARK

Plate 319. Pompey shade. Ribbed. *Peonies pink and red on green and white background* decoration #934. Base #B3041. 1910-1914.

No. B 3038. ELECTROLIER, with 8 Feet Silk Cord. Height of Body, 14 inches.
One Light, Less Shade, Old Brass Green, Gun Metal or Antique, $17.00   Two Lights, $21.00

THE PAIRPOINT CORPORATION.
NEW BEDFORD, MASS.
38 Murray Street, New York City.
Coristine Building, St. Nicholas St.,
Montreal, Canada.
717 Market St., San Francisco, Cal.
NEG. 969 A

No. 901 A   14 inch Pompey Shade, $10.00

Plate 320. Pompey shade. Ribbed. *Yellow wild roses with leaves on stippled background* decoration #901A. Base #B3038. 1910-1914.

Plate 321. Pompey shade. Ribbed. *Floral wreath with ribbon* decoration #692. Base #B3053 1/2. No date.

Plate 322. Pompey shade. Ribbed. *Moonlight harbor scene* decoration #544. Base #B3055 1/2. No date.

No. B 3059.   ELECTROLIER, with 8 Feet Silk Cord.   Height of Body, 13½ inches.

One Light, Less Shade, Plain Old Brass Green, Gun Metal or Antique, $12.50   Two Light, $16.50
Engraved Old Brass Green, or Gun Metal.   13.50   "   17.50
Fancy Coloring, $1.00 extra.
No. 531   14 inch Pompey Shade, $9.00

THE PAIRPOINT CORPORATION,
NEW BEDFORD, MASS.
38 Murray Street, New York City.
Coristine Building, St. Nicholas St.,
Montreal, Canada.
717 Market St., San Francisco, Cal.
NEG. 953 A

TRADE MARK

Plate 323. Pompey shade. Ribbed. *Mallards in flight* decoration #531. Base #B3059. 1910-1914.

No. B 3067. ELECTROLIER, with 8 Feet Silk Cord. Height of Body, 12 inches.
One Light, Less Shade, Plain Old Brass, Gun Metal or Antique, $10.00 Two Light, $14.00
" " Engraved Old Brass, or Gun Metal, 12.00 " 16.00
Fancy Coloring, $1.50 extra

THE PAIRPOINT CORPORATION,
NEW BEDFORD, MASS.
38 Murray Street, New York City.
Coristine Building, St. Nicholas St.,
Montreal, Canada.
717 Market St., San Francisco, Cal.

No. 902 A. 14 inch Pompey Shade, $10.00

TRADE MARK

Plate 324. Pompey shade. Ribbed. *Pond lilies* decoration #902A. Base #B3067. 1910-1914.

Plate 325. Pond lily shade. Puffy. *Pond lily with dragonfly* decoration #898. Base #B3021; Bristol shade. Puffy. *Floral* decoration #899. Base #D3007 (mahogany). 1915.

Plate 326. Poppy shade. Puffy. *Three color* decoration #690. Base #3049 (Poppy base). No date.

PATENTED JULY 9, 1907.

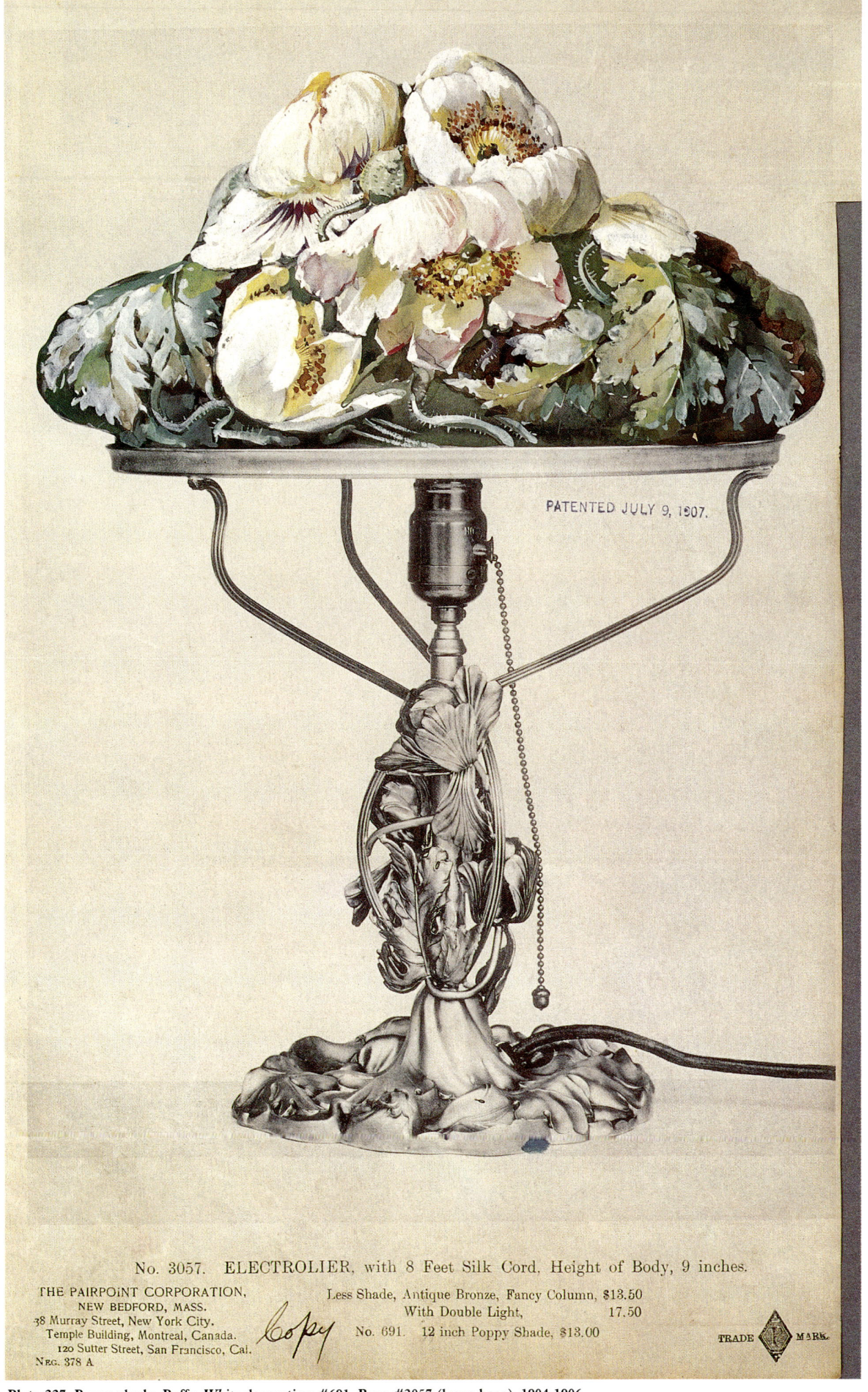

No. 3057. ELECTROLIER, with 8 Feet Silk Cord. Height of Body, 9 inches.

THE PAIRPOINT CORPORATION,
NEW BEDFORD, MASS.
38 Murray Street, New York City.
Temple Building, Montreal, Canada.
120 Sutter Street, San Francisco, Cal.
NEG. 378 A

Less Shade, Antique Bronze, Fancy Column, $13.50
With Double Light, 17.50
No. 691. 12 inch Poppy Shade, $13.00

TRADE MARK

Plate 327. Poppy shade. Puffy. *White* decoration #691. Base #3057 (leave base). 1904-1906.

Plate 328. Poppy shade. Puffy. *Three color* decoration #690. Base #3085. No date.

No. 3047½.   ELECTROLIER, with 8 Feet Silk Cord, Height of Body, 8 inches.

THE PAIRPOINT CORPORATION,
NEW BEDFORD, MASS.
38 Murray Street, New York City.
485 St. Catherine St., Montreal, Canada.
717 Market St., San Francisco, Cal.
Neg. 579 A

Less Shade, Plain, Old Brass, $7.50
    "   Engraved, Old Brass,   8.50
No. 1387. 8 inch Portsmouth Shade,   5.00

TRADE MARK

Plate 329. Portsmouth shade. *Flemish Clematis* decoration #1387. Base #3047 1/2. 1907-1910.

Plate 330. Portsmouth shade. *Flemish wisteria* decoration #1359. Base #B3007. 1907

No. B 3057. ELECTROLIER, with 8 Feet Silk Cord, Height of Body, 15½ inches.

THE PAIRPOINT CORPORATION,
NEW BEDFORD, MASS.
38 Murray Street, New York City.
485 St. Catherine St., Montreal, Canada.
717 Market St., San Francisco, Cal.
NEG 769 A

Less Shade, Old Brass, Antique Green, Gun Metal or Copper, $17.00
Two Lights, $4.00 extra.
No. 976. 14 inch Ravenna Shade, $20.00

Plate 340. Ravenna shade. Puffy. *Floral with stripes* decoration #976. Base #B3057. 1907-1910.

Plate 339. Ravenna shade. Puffy. *Floral tapestry* decoration #974. Base #B3056. No date.

No. 3099. ELECTROLIER, with 8 Feet Silk Cord, Height of Body, 14 inches.

THE PAIRPOINT CORPORATION.
NEW BEDFORD, MASS.
38 Murray Street, New York City.
485 St. Catherine St., Montreal, Canada.
717 Market St., San Francisco, Cal.
NEG. 796 A

Less Shade, Old Brass, Antique Green, Gun Metal or Copper, $15.00

Two Lights, $4.00 extra.

No. 538. 18 inch Ravenna Shade, $30.00

Plate 338. Ravenna shade. Puffy. *Flying cherub with flowers* decoration #538. Base #3099. No date.

No. C 3077. ELECTROLIER, with 8 Feet Silk Cord, Height of Body, 9 inches.

THE PAIRPOINT CORPORATION,
NEW BEDFORD, MASS.
38 Murray Street, New York City.
Coristine Building, St. Nicholas St.,
Montreal, Canada.
717 Market St., San Francisco, Cal.
NEG. 518

One Light, Less Shade, Engraved, Old Brass Green, $5.90
No. 755. 8 inch Portsmouth Shade, $4.55

TRADE MARK.

Plate 337. Portsmouth shade. *Woodland cabin* decoration #755. Base #C3077. 1910-1914.

No. C 3059. ELECTROLIER, with 8 Feet Silk Cord, Height of Body, 9 inches.
Plain, One Light, Less Shade, Old Brass Green, Antique or Gun Metal, $7.75

THE PAIRPOINT CORPORATION,
NEW BEDFORD, MASS.
38 Murray Street, New York City.
Coristine Building, St. Nicholas St.,
Montreal, Canada.
717 Market St., San Francisco, Cal.

No. 668. 8 inch Portsmouth Shade, $4.10

Plate 336. Portsmouth shade. *Robin with spring flowers* decoration #668. Base #C3059. 1910-1914.

No. C 3053.   ELECTROLIER, with 8 Feet Silk Cord, Height of Body, 8 inches.
Plain.   One Light, Less Shade, Old Brass, Antique or Gun Metal, $9.55
Engraved, "   "   "   "   "   "   "   Green   "   "   10.95
"   "   "   "   "   "   French Grey, $10.50
"   "   "   "   "   Engraved, French Gray, 11.85

THE PAIRPOINT CORPORATION,
NEW BEDFORD, MASS.
38 Murray Street, New York City.
Coristine Building, St. Nicholas St.,
Montreal, Canada.
717 Market St., San Francisco, Cal.
NEG. 483

Fancy Coloring, $ .95 Extra.

No. 503. 8 inch Portsmouth Shade, $4.55

TRADE P M

Plate 335. Portsmouth shade. *Egyptian* decoration #503. Base #C3053. 1910-1914.

No. B 3045.   ELECTROLIER, with 8 Feet Silk Cord, Height of Body, 7 inches.

THE PAIRPOINT CORPORATION,
NEW BEDFORD, MASS.
38 Murray Street, New York City.
485 St. Catherine St., Montreal, Canada.
717 Market St., San Francisco, Cal.
NEG. 647 A

Less Shade, Copper, Gray Finish, $7.50
No. 1550. 8 inch Portsmouth Shade, $6.00

Plate 334. Portsmouth shade. *Antique lace* decoration #1550. Base #B3045. 1907-1910.

No. B 3025. **ELECTROLIER**, with 8 Feet Silk Cord, Height of Body, 8½ inches.

THE PAIRPOINT CORPORATION,
NEW BEDFORD, MASS.
38 Murray Street, New York City.
485 St. Catherine St., Montreal, Canada.
717 Market St., San Francisco, Cal.
NEG 730 A

Less Shade, Old Brass, $7.00
No. 1368. 8 inch Portsmouth Shade, $5.00

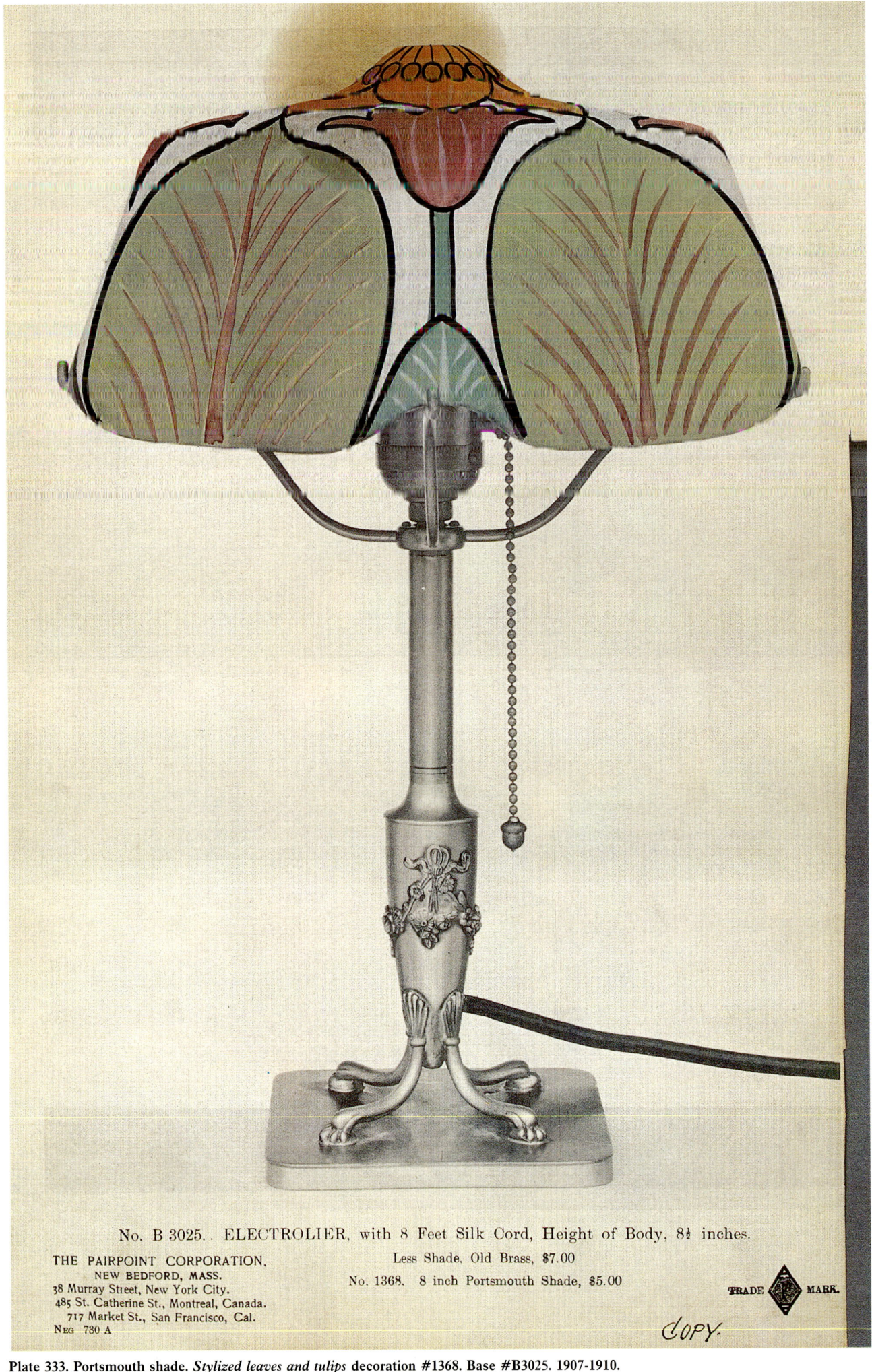

TRADE MARK

COPY.

Plate 333. Portsmouth shade. *Stylized leaves and tulips* decoration #1368. Base #B3025. 1907-1910.

No. B 3023. ELECTROLIER, with 8 Feet Silk Cord, Height of Body, 8 inches.

THE PAIRPOINT CORPORATION.
NEW BEDFORD, MASS.
38 Murray Street, New York City.
36 St. Antoine St., Montreal, Canada.
717 Market St., San Francisco, Cal.
Neg. 520 A

Less Shade, Plain, Old Brass, $6.00
" Engraved, " 7.50
No. 1380. 8 inch Portsmouth Shade, $5.00

TRADE MARK

Plate 332. Portsmouth shade. *Wild roses with white and green panels* decoration #1380. Base #B3023. 1907.

No. B 3021.   ELECTROLIER, with 8 Feet Silk Cord, Height of Body, 6½ inches.

THE PAIRPOINT CORPORATION,
NEW BEDFORD, MASS.
38 Murray Street, New York City.
Coristine Building, St. Nicholas St.,
Montreal, Canada.
717 Market St., San Francisco, Cal.
NEG. 521

One Light, Less Shade, Plain, Old Brass Green, $5.50
No. 754. 8 inch Portsmouth Shade, $5.90

TRADE MARK

Plate 331. Portsmouth shade. *Orchids on mottled background* **decoration #754. Base #B3021. 1910-1914.**

No. C 6121. CANDLE. Height of Body, 5½ inches.
With Electric Candle Fittings.
Plain Silver, $5.00
No. 1218. 5 inch Resina Shade, $1.85

THE PAIRPOINT CORPORATION,
NEW BEDFORD, MASS.
18 Murray Street, New York City.
Coristine Building, St. Nicholas St.,
Montreal, Canada.
717 Market St., San Francisco, Cal.

No. C 6122. CANDLE. Height of Body, 5½ inches.
With Electric Candle Fittings.
Plain Silver, $5.50
No. 1212. 5 inch Cremona Shade, $1.85

QUADRUPLE PLATE

No. C 6123. CANDLE. Height of Body, 6 inches.
With Electric Candle Fittings.
Plain Silver, $5.90
No. 1244. 5 inch Carmela Shade, $1.85

TRADE MARK

Above: Plate 341. Candlestick lamps. Resina shades. *Stylized daisy* decoration #1218. Base #C6121; Cremona shade. *Wreath and bow* decoration #1212. Base #C6122; Carmelia shade. Ribbed. *Poppy tapestry* decoration #1244. Base #C6123. 1910-1914.

Below: Plate 342. Resina shade. *Stylized floral* decoration #1217; *Stylized floral with lace stripes* decoration #1211; Carmela shade. *Greek key with fleur-de-lys* decoration #1210; *Poppy tapestry* decoration #1209. 1910-1914.

No. 1217. 5 inch Resina Shade, $1.85

No. 1211. 5 inch Resina Shade, $1.85

No. 1210. 5 inch Carmela Shade, $2.30

No. 1209. 5 inch Carmela Shade, $1.85

THE PAIRPOINT CORPORATION,
NEW BEDFORD, MASS.
18 Murray Street, New York City.
Coristine Building, St. Nicholas St.,
Montreal, Canada.
717 Market St., San Francisco, Cal.

DECORATED SHADES.

TRADE MARK

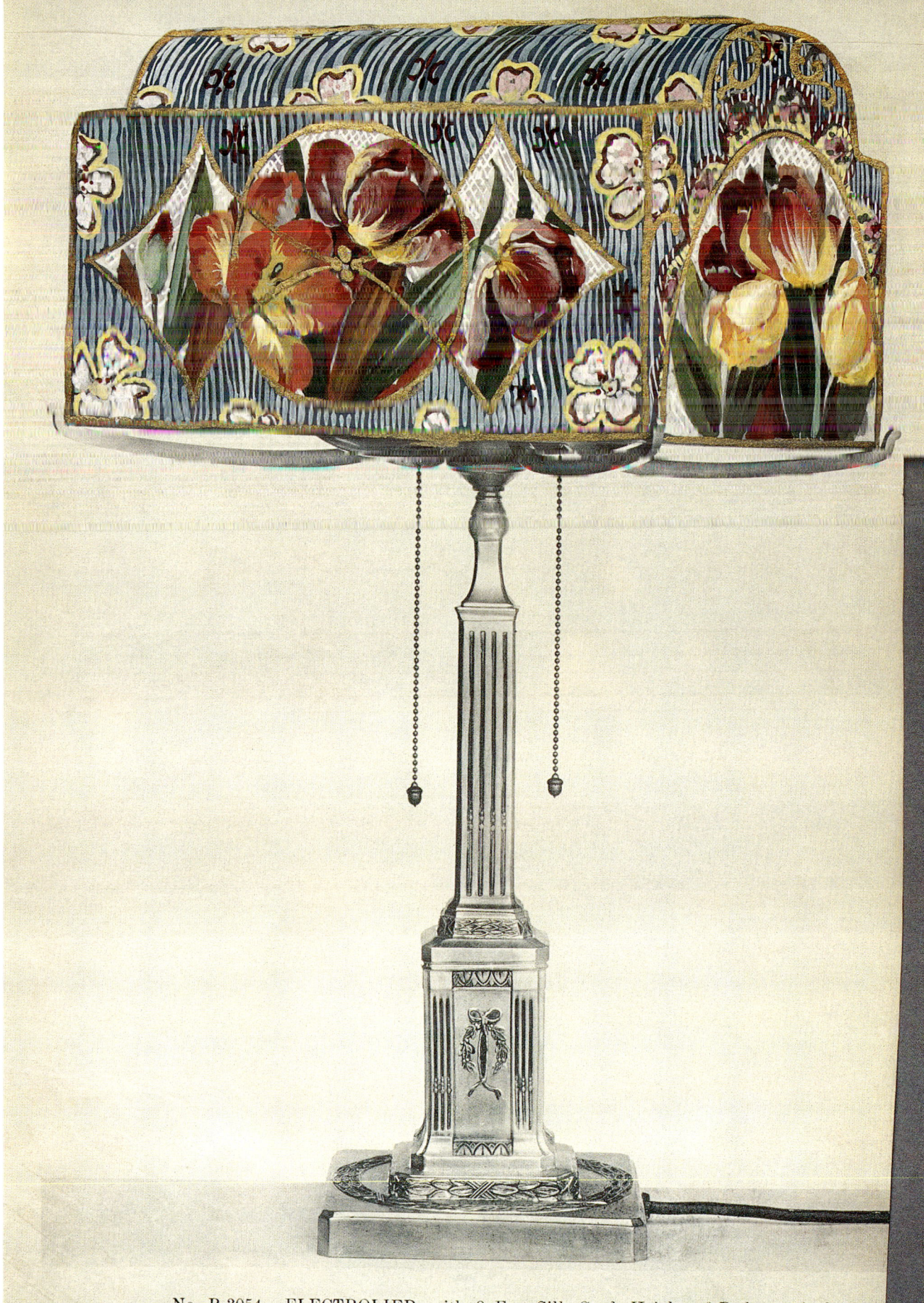

No. B 3054. ELECTROLIER, with 8 Feet Silk Cord, Height of Body, 15 inches.

THE PAIRPOINT CORPORATION,
NEW BEDFORD, MASS.
38 Murray Street, New York City.
485 St. Catherine St., Montreal, Canada.
717 Market St., San Francisco, Cal.
NEG 767 A

Less Shade, Old Brass, Antique or Copper, Green, $20.00
Two Lights, $4.00 extra.
No. 972. 18 inch Roma Shade, $20.00

Plate 343. Roma shade. *Tulips with turquoise background* decoration #972. Base #B3054. 1907-1910.

No. B 3055.   ELECTROLIER, with 8 Feet Silk Cord, Height of Body, 14 inches.
Less Shade, Old Brass, Antique Green, Gun Metal or Copper, $19.00
Fancy Inlaid, $21.00
Two Lights, $4.00 extra.
No. 530.   18 inch Roma Shade, $30.00

THE PAIRPOINT CORPORATION.
NEW BEDFORD, MASS.
38 Murray Street, New York City.
485 St. Catherine St., Montreal, Canada.
717 Market St., San Francisco, Cal.
NEG 800 A

Plate 344. Roma shade. *Venetian gondola* decoration #530. Base #B3055. 1907-1910.

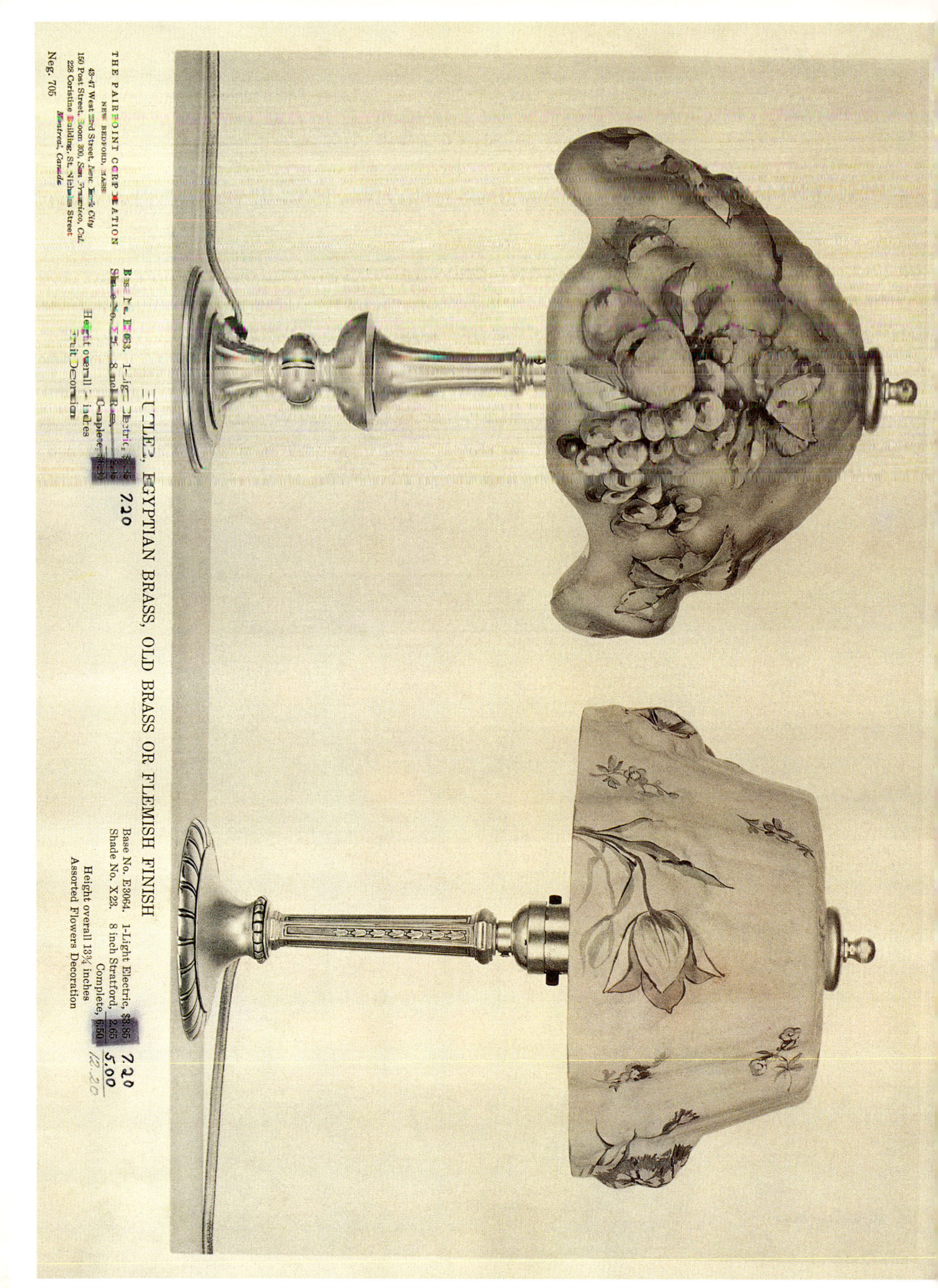

Plate 345. Rose shade. Puffy. Fruit Decoration #X26. Base #E3063; Stratford shade. Puffy. Assorted Flowers Decoration #X23. Base #E3064. 1930.

No. C 3023.   ELECTROLIER, with 8 Feet Silk Cord.   Height of Body, 9 inches.

Plain,   One Light, Old Brass, Antique or Gun Metal, $10.50
Engraved,   "   "   "   "   "   "   "   12.00
Plain Silver, $11.50
Eng.   "   13.00
Fancy Coloring, $1.50 extra.

No. 617.   Pink Rose,
No. 618.   White   "   } 8 inch Shade, $7.00

THE PAIRPOINT CORPORATION,
NEW BEDFORD, MASS.
38 Murray Street, New York City.
Coristine Building, St. Nicholas St.,
Montreal, Canada.
717 Market St., San Francisco, Cal.
Neg. 277

Plate 346. Rose shade. Puffy. *Pink bouquet* decoration #617. Base #C3023. 1910-1914.

No. C 3018.   ELECTROLIER, with 8 Feet Silk Cord.   Height of Body, 14 inches.

One Light, Less Shade, Old Brass Green, Antique or Gun Metal, $13.50   Two Lights, $16.25

THE PAIRPOINT CORPORATION,
NEW BEDFORD, MASS.

No. 951.   12 inch Rose Shade, $15.00

38 Murray Street, New York City.
Coristine Building, St. Nicholas St.,
Montreal, Canada.
717 Market St., San Francisco, Cal.

NEG. 241

TRADE

Plate 347. Rose shade. *Puffy. Bonnet with butterfly, rose* decoration #951. Base #C3018. 1910-1914.

ELECTROLIERS, with 8 Feet Silk Cord.

THE PAIRPOINT CORPORATION,
NEW BEDFORD, MASS.
18 Murray Street, New York City.
Coristine Building, St. Nicholas St.,
Montreal, Canada.
717 Market St., San Francisco, Cal.

No. B 3079. Height of Body, 7 inches.
One Light, Less Shade, Plain Old Brass Green, Antique or Gun Metal, $5.00
No. 951. 5 inch Red Rose Shade, } $3.00
" 952. 5 " White "

No. B 3080. Height of Body, 7 inches.
One Light, Less Shade, Plain Old Brass Green, Antique or Gun Metal, $5.00
No. 645. 8 in. Pond Lily Shade, $3.50

Above: Plate 348. Rose shade. Puffy. *Roses with butterfly, red* decoration #951. Base #B3079 (tree trunk); Pond lily shade. Puffy. *Pond lily* decoration #645. Base #B3080. 1910-1914.

Below: Plate 349. Rose shade. Puffy. *Roses with butterfly, red* decoration #951. Base #B3088 (potted with tree trunk); Lotus shade. *Banana/Palm* decoration #684. Base #B3086 (potted with trunk). 1910-1914.

ELECTROLIERS. With 8 Feet Silk Cord.

THE PAIRPOINT CORPORATION,
NEW BEDFORD, MASS.
18 Murray Street, New York City.
Coristine Building, St. Nicholas St.,
Montreal, Canada.
717 Market St., San Francisco, Cal.

No. B 3088. Height of Body, 7 inches.
Less Shade, Old Brass Green, Antique or Gun Metal, $6.50
No. 951. 5 inch Red Rose Shade, } $3.00
" 952. 5 " White "

No. B 3086. Height of Body, 7 inches.
Less Shade, Old Brass Green, Antique or Gun Metal, $6.00
No. 684. 5 inch Lotus Shade, $3.00

No. 3095. ELECTROLIER, with 8 Feet Silk Cord, Height of Body, 12 inches.

THE PAIRPOINT CORPORATION,
NEW BEDFORD, MASS.
38 Murray Street, New York City.
36 St. Antoine St., Montreal, Canada.
717 Market St., San Francisco, Cal.
NEG. 412 A

No. 610. 10 inch Rose Shade, $13.00

Two Lights, 17.00

TRADE MARK

Plate 350. Rose shade. Puffy. *White* decoration #610. Base #3095 (sculpted). 1907.

No. B 3089. ELECTROLIER. With 8 Feet Silk Cord, Height of Body, 10 inches.

THE PAIRPOINT CORPORATION,
NEW BEDFORD, MASS.
38 Murray Street, New York City.
Coristine Building, St. Nicholas St.,
Montreal, Canada.
717 Market St., San Francisco, Cal.
NEG 49

One Light, Less Shade, Old Brass Green, Antique or Gun Metal, $10.00
No. 951. 8 inch, Red Rose Shade,
" 952. 8 " White " } $8.00

TRADE M.

Plate 351. Rose shade. Puffy. Red decoration #951. Base #B3089 (potted with tree trunk). 1910-1914.

THE PAIRPOINT CORPORATION,
NEW BEDFORD, MASS.
43-47 West 23d St., New York City.
402 Columbus Memoria. Bldg., Chicago.
140 Geary St., San Francisco, Cal.
Coristine Building, St. Nicholas St.,
Montreal, Canada

ELECTROLIERS. With 7 Feet Silk Cord and Push Button Sockets.

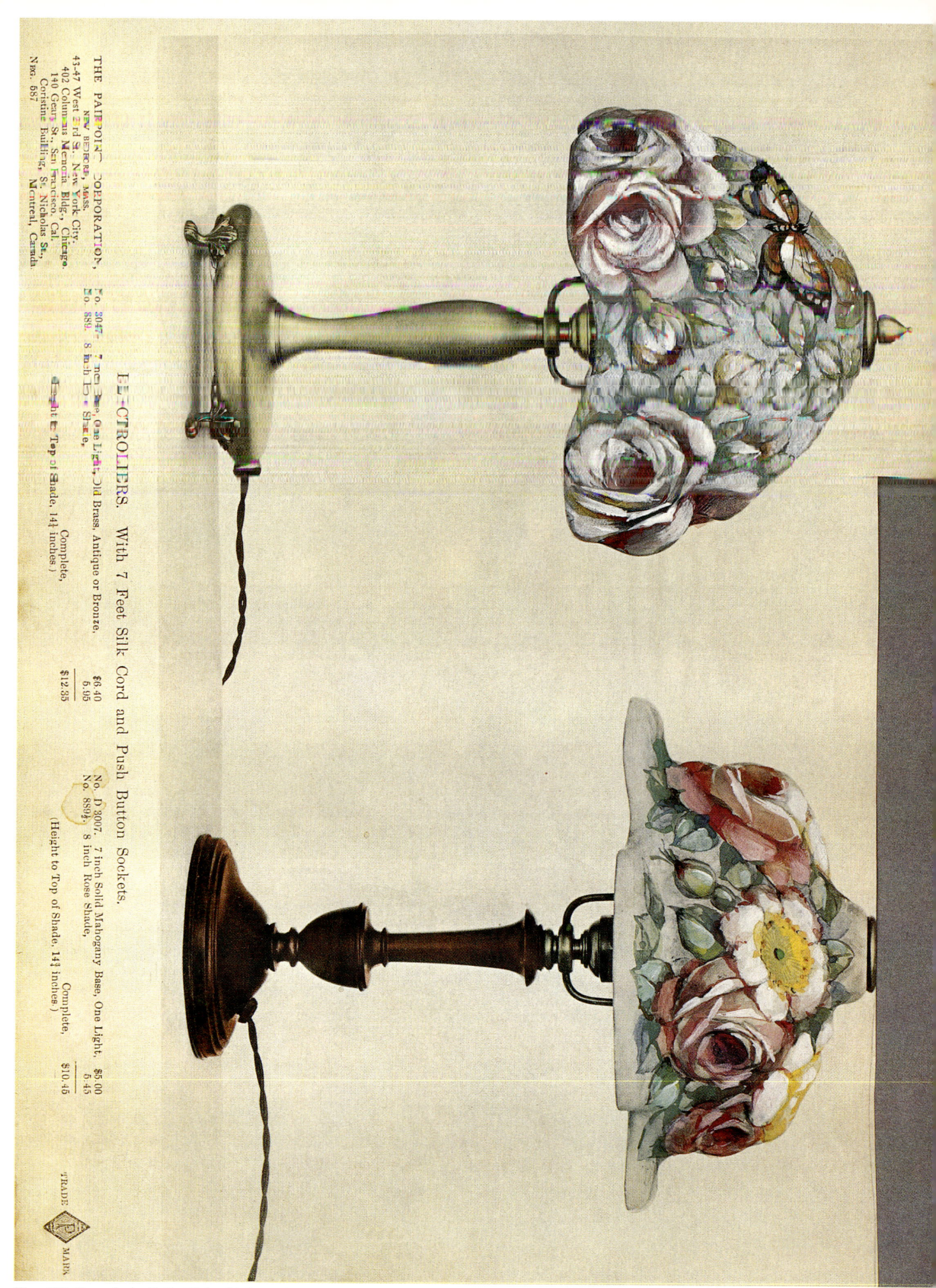

No. 3047 ½, 7 inch Tree, One Light, Old Brass, Antique or Bronze. $6.40
No. 889, 8 inch B. Shade, 5.95
Complete, $12.35
(Height to Top of Shade, 14½ inches.)

No. D 3007, 7 inch Solid Mahogany Base, One Light, $5.00
No. 889½, 8 inch Rose Shade, 5.45
Complete, $10.45
(Height to Top of Shade, 14½ inches.)

TRADE MARK

Plate 352. Rose shade. Puffy. *Pink with butterflies* decoration #889 (open top). Base #3047 1/2; Rose shade. Puffy. *Roses, pink* decoration #889 1/2 (open top). Base #D3007(mahogany). 1915.

No. B 3053. ELECTROLIER, with 8 Feet Silk Cord, Height of Body, 15 inches.

THE PAIRPOINT CORPORATION.
NEW BEDFORD, MASS.
38 Murray Street, New York City.
485 St. Catherine St., Montreal, Canada.
717 Market St., San Francisco, Cal.
Neg 765 A

Less Shade, Old Brass, Antique Green, Gun Metal, or Copper, $19.00
Fancy Inlaid, $21.00
Two Lights, $4.00 extra.
No. 932. 16 inch San Reno Shade, $18.00 (PINK MARBLE)
No 933. 16 inch San Reno Shade as above, Green Marble Decoration, $18.00

Plate 353. San Reno shade. Puffy. *Pansies, roses on pink marble background* **decoration #932. Base #B3053. 1907-1910.**

Plate 354. San Reno shade. Puffy. *Yellow and pink roses decoration* #922. Base #B3054. No date.

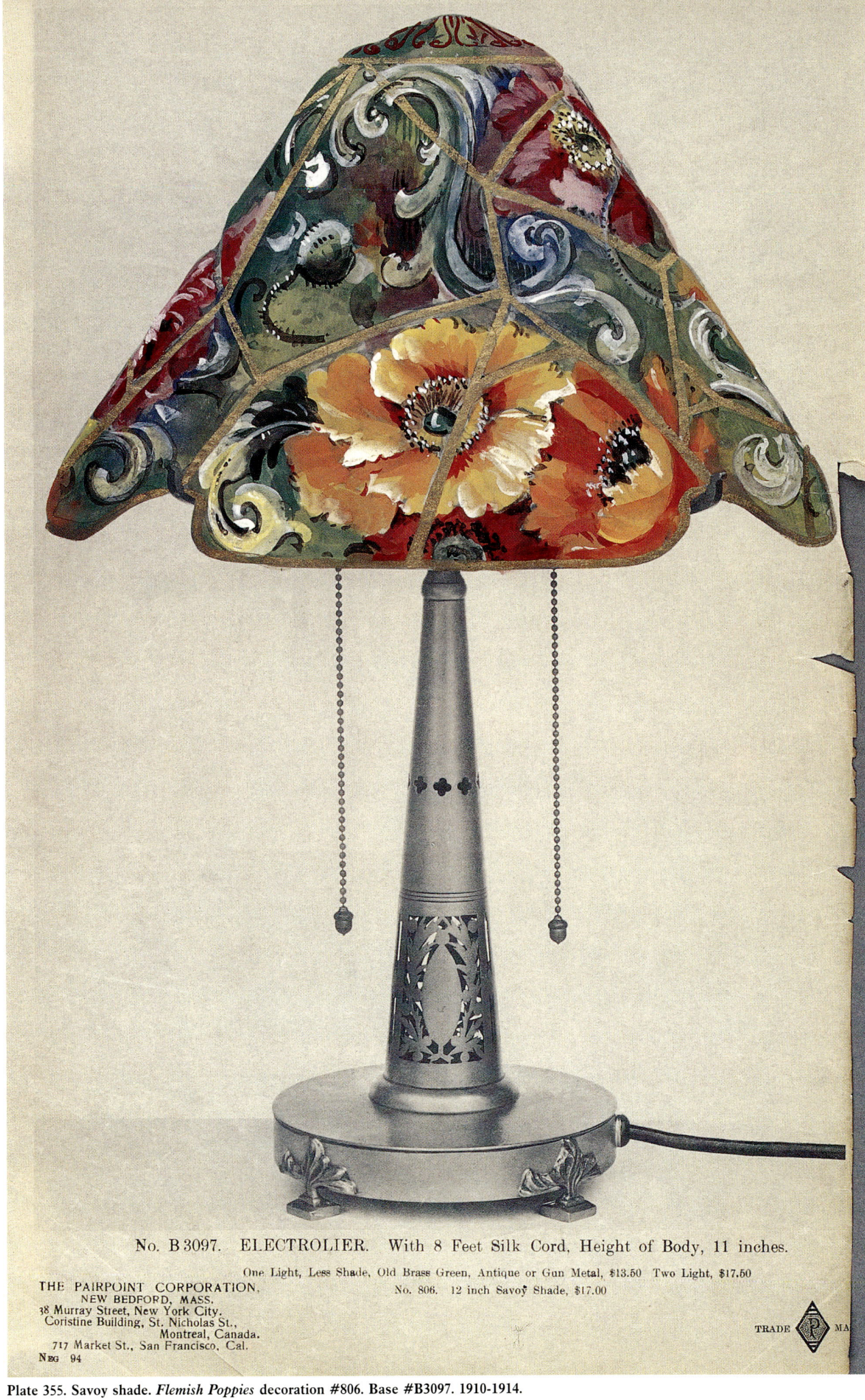

No. B 3097. ELECTROLIER. With 8 Feet Silk Cord, Height of Body, 11 inches.
One Light, Less Shade, Old Brass Green, Antique or Gun Metal, $13.50   Two Light, $17.50
No. 806.   12 inch Savoy Shade, $17.00

THE PAIRPOINT CORPORATION,
NEW BEDFORD, MASS.
38 Murray Street, New York City.
Coristine Building, St. Nicholas St.,
Montreal, Canada.
717 Market St., San Francisco, Cal.

Plate 355. Savoy shade. *Flemish Poppies* decoration #806. Base #B3097. 1910-1914.

No. C 3002.   ELECTROLIER.   With 8 Feet Silk Cord, Height of Body, 11 inches.

THE PAIRPOINT CORPORATION,
NEW BEDFORD, MASS.
38 Murray Street, New York City.
Coristine Building, St. Nicholas St.,
Montreal, Canada.
717 Market St., San Francisco, Cal.

NEG 69

One Light. Less Shade, Old Brass, Antique Green or Gun Metal, $14.50
Two   "   "   "   "   "   "   "   "   "   18.50

No. 815. 12 inch Savoy Shade, $13.00

TRADE

Plate 356. Savoy shade. *Flemish Roses* decoration #815. Base #C3002. 1910-1914.

No. B 3050. ELECTROLIER, with 8 Feet Silk Cord, Height of Body, 9½ inches.

THE PAIRPOINT CORPORATION.
NEW BEDFORD, MASS.
38 Murray Street, New York City.
485 St. Catherine St., Montreal, Canada.
717 Market St., San Francisco, Cal.
NEG 716 A

Less Shade, Old Brass or Antique, $9.00
No.   10 inch Sorento Shade, 7.00

Plate 357. Sorento shade. Puffy. *Roses with green stripes* decoration #951. Base #B3050. 1907-1910.

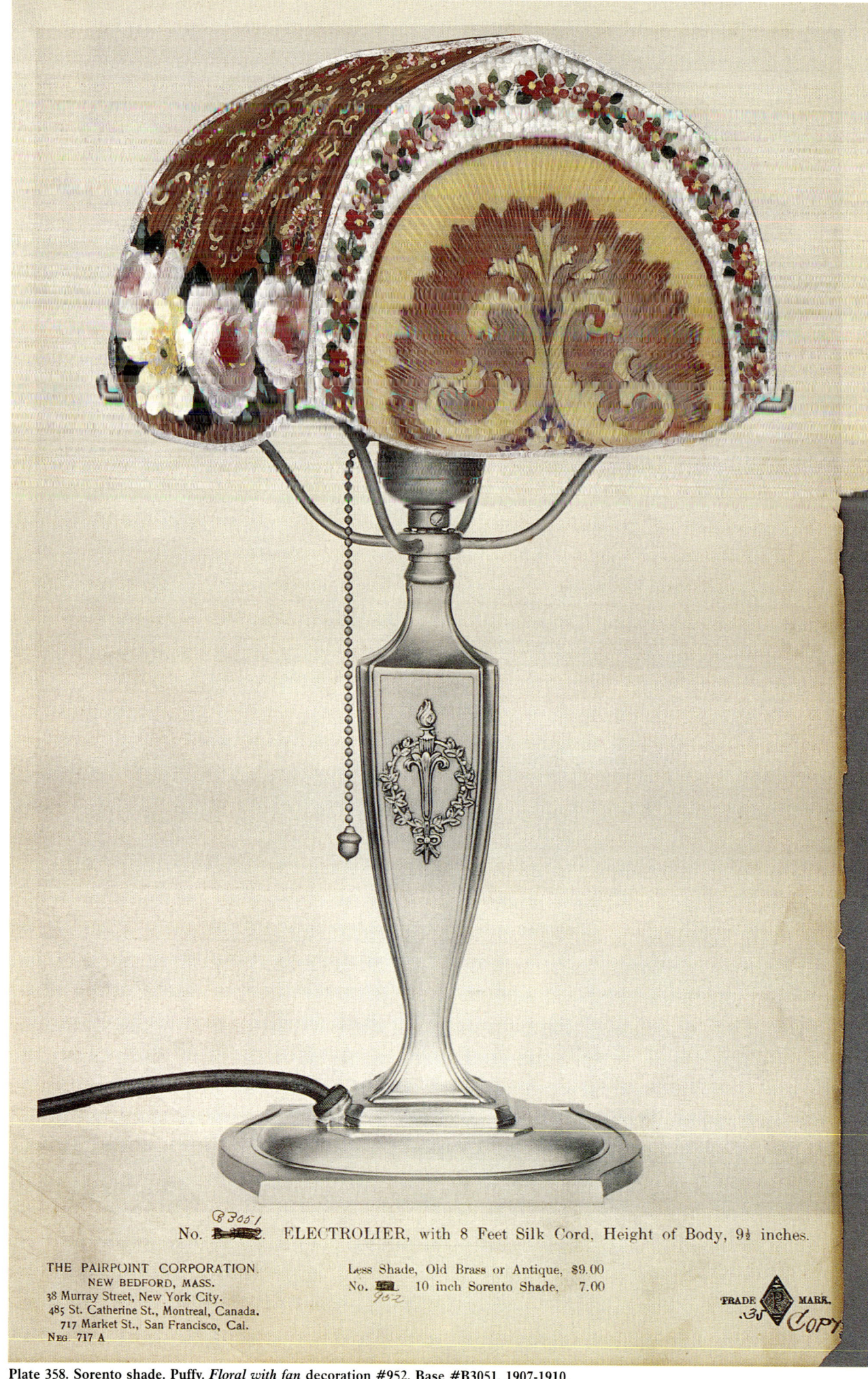

No. B3051   ELECTROLIER, with 8 Feet Silk Cord, Height of Body, 9½ inches.

THE PAIRPOINT CORPORATION
NEW BEDFORD, MASS.
38 Murray Street, New York City.
485 St. Catherine St., Montreal, Canada.
717 Market St., San Francisco, Cal.
NEG. 717 A

Less Shade, Old Brass or Antique, $9.00
No. 952   10 inch Sorento Shade,   7.00

Plate 358. Sorento shade. Puffy. *Floral with fan* **decoration #952. Base #B3051. 1907-1910.**

No. C 3032. ELECTROLIER, with 8 Feet Silk Cord. Height of Body, 9½ inches.

THE PAIRPOINT CORPORATION,
NEW BEDFORD, MASS.
38 Murray Street, New York City.
Coristine Building, St. Nicholas St.,
Montreal, Canada.
717 Market St., San Francisco, Cal.
NEG 281

Marble Base.
One Light, Less Shade, Old Brass, Antique or Gun Metal, $7.00
No. 957. 10 inch Sorento Shade. $7.00

TRADE

Plate 359. Sorento shade. Puffy. *Pleated drape with fan, roses on sides* decoration #957. Base #C3032. 1910-1914.

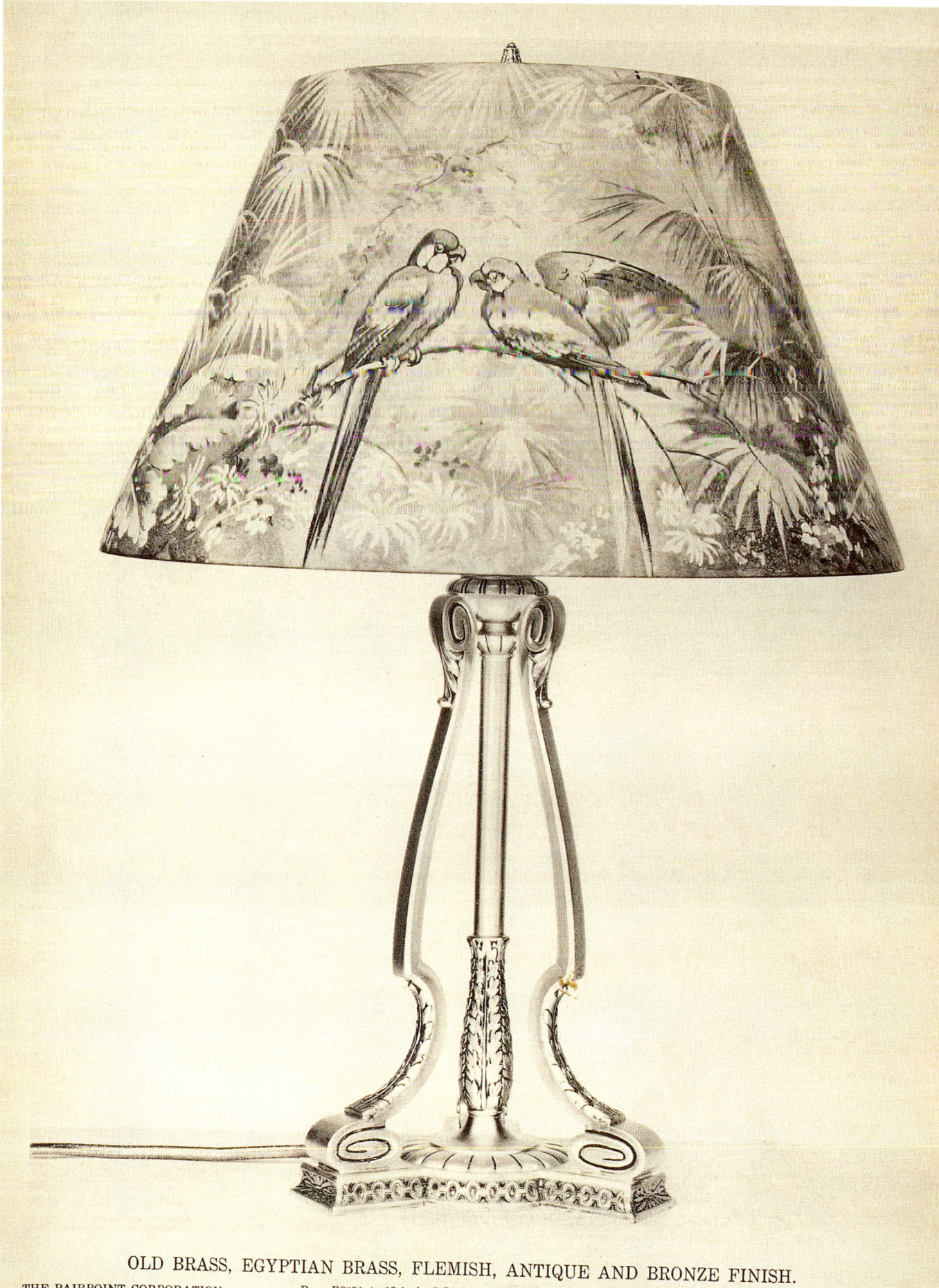

OLD BRASS, EGYPTIAN BRASS, FLEMISH, ANTIQUE AND BRONZE FINISH.

THE PAIRPOINT CORPORATION.
NEW BEDFORD, MASS.
43-47 West 23rd St., New York City.
Hammond Bldg., 278 Post St.,
San Francisco, Cal.
228 Coristine Building, St. Nicholas St.,
NEG. 8   Montreal, Can.

		Butler Silver,
Base D3084½—12 inch, 2 Light,	$15.00	$16.80
14 inch Seville Shade, No. 471	12.00	12.00
Decoration: Parrots.	$27.00	$28.80
Height Overall, 21½ inches.		
Base D3084½—12 inch, 2 Light,	$15.00	$16.80
16 inch Seville Shade, No. 471	16.70	16.70
Height Overall, 22 inches.	$31.70	$33.50

Plate 360. Seville shade. Parrots decoration #471. Base #D3084 1/2. 1926.

OLD BRASS, EGYPTIAN BRASS, FLEMISH, ANTIQUE AND BRONZE FINISH.

THE PAIRPOINT CORPORATION.
NEW BEDFORD, MASS.
43-47 West 23rd St., New York City.
Hammond Bldg., 278 Post St.,
San Francisco, Cal.
228 Coristine Building, St. Nicholas St.,
Neg. 9   Montreal, Can.

Base D3076½. 12 inch, 2 Light,
16 inch Seville Shade, No. 564,

Butler Silver,

Decoration: Western Ocean.

Height Overall 22 inches.

Plate 361. Seville shade. Western Ocean decoration #564. Base #D3076 1/2. 1926.

OLD BRASS, EGYPTIAN BRASS, FLEMISH, ANTIQUE AND BRONZE FINISH.

THE PAIRPOINT CORPORATION.
NEW BEDFORD, MASS
43-47 West 23rd St., New York City.
Hammond Bldg., 278 Post St., San Francisco, Cal.
228 Coristine Building, St. Nicholas St., Montreal, Can.
Neg. 12

Base D3084 1/2—12 inch, 2 Light.........$13.65   Butler Silver, $15.45
16 inch Seville Shade, No. 563............ 17.30   17.30
Decoration: Urn with Flowers. $30.95 $32.75
Height Overall, 22 inches.

Plate 362. Seville shade. Urn with Flowers decoration #563. Base #D3084 1/2. 1926.

OLD BRASS, EGYPTIAN BRASS, FLEMISH, ANTIQUE AND BRONZE FINISH.

THE PAIRPOINT CORPORATION
NEW BEDFORD, MASS.
43-47 West 23rd St., New York City.
228 Coristine Building, St. Nicholas St.,
NEG. 77   Montreal, Can.

Base D3095½. 2 Light,	$22.30	Butler Silver,	$24.10
16 inch Seville Shade No. 226,	20.00	Shade,	20.00
	$42.30		$44.10

Decoration: Tapestry.
Lamps equipped with Alps Green Marble Base
Height Overall 22½ inches.

Plate 363. Seville shade. Tapestry decoration #226. Base #D3095 1/2 (Alps green marble). 1926 (?)-1930.

OLD BRASS, EGYPTIAN BRASS, FLEMISH, ANTIQUE AND BRONZE FINISH.

THE PAIRPOINT CORPORATION,
NEW BEDFORD, MASS
43-47 West 23rd St., New York City.
Hammond Bldg., 278 Post St.,
San Francisco, Cal.
228 Coristine Building, St. Nicholas St.,
NEG. 117   Montreal, Can.

Base D3075½, 12 inch, 2 Light, $14.00
14 inch Seville Shade, No. 559,   14.65
$28.65

Butler Silver, $15.80
14.65
$30.45

Decoration: Green Border Sevres.
Height Overall 21¾ inches.

Plate 364. Seville shade. Green Border Sevres decoration #559. Base #D3075 1/2. 1926.

OLD BRASS, EGYPTIAN BRASS, FLEMISH, ANTIQUE AND BRONZE FINISH.

THE PAIRPOINT CORPORATION
NEW BEDFORD, MASS.
43-47 West 23rd St., New York City
228 Coristine Building, St. Nicholas St.,
Neg. 161   Montreal, Can.

Base D3084½. 12 inch. 2 Light, $15.00   Butler Silver, $16.80
16 inch Seville Shade No. 223,   18.65   Shade,   18.65
                                   $33.65 $35.45

Decoration: Canterbury.
Height Overall 22 inches.

Plate 365. Seville shade. Canterbury decoration #223. Base #D3084 1/2. 1926(?)-1930.

OLD BRASS, EGYPTIAN BRASS, FLEMISH, ANTIQUE AND BRONZE FINISH.

THE PAIRPOINT CORPORATION
NEW BEDFORD, MASS.
43-47 West 23rd St., New York City
228 Coristine Building, St. Nicholas St.,
NEG. 271   Montreal, Can.

Base D3084½. 12 inch. 2 Light,	$15.00	Butler Silver,	$16.80
16 inch Seville Shade No. 225,	18.65	Shade,	18.65
	$33.65		$35.45

Decoration: Cedars.
Height Overall 22 inches.

Plate 366. Seville shade. Cedars decoration #225. Base #D3084 1/2. 1926-1930.

OLD BRASS, EGYPTIAN BRASS, FLEMISH, ANTIQUE AND BRONZE FINISH.

THE PAIRPOINT CORPORATION.
NEW BEDFORD, MASS.
83-47 West 23rd St., New York City.
Hammond Bldg., 278 Post St.,
San Francisco, Cal.
228 Coristine Building, St. Nicholas St.,
NEG. 281   Montreal, Can.

Base D3070½. 2 Light,	$13.65	Butler Silver,	$15.45
18 inch Seville Shade, No. 264	24.00		24.00
	$37.65		$39.45

Base D3070½. 3 Light,	$15.00	Butler Silver	$16.80
18 inch Seville Shade, No. 264	24.00		24.00
	$39.00		$40.80

Decoration: The Capital.
Height Overall 24 inches.

Plate 367. Seville shade. The Capital decoration #264. Base #D3070 1/2. 1926.

OLD BRASS,   EGYPTIAN BRASS,   FLEMISH,   ANTIQUE AND BRONZE FINISH.

| THE PAIRPOINT CORPORATION. NEW BEDFORD, MASS. 83-47 West 23rd St., New York City. Hammond Bldg., 278 Post St., San Francisco, Cal. 228 Coristine Building, St. Nicholas St., Montreal, Can. NEG. 282 | Base D3084½. 2 Light, 18 inch Seville Shade, No. 265 | $13.65 22.00 $35.65 | Butler Silver, | $15.45 22.00 $37.45 | Base D3084½. 3 Light, 18 inch Seville Shade, No. 265 | $15.00 22.00 $37.00 | Butler Silver | $16.80 22.00 $38.80 |

Decoration: New England.
Height Overall 23 inches.

Plate 368. Seville shade. New England decoration #265. Base #D3084 1/2. 1926.

OLD BRASS, EGYPTIAN BRASS, FLEMISH, ANTIQUE AND BRONZE FINISH.

THE PAIRPOINT CORPORATION.
NEW BEDFORD, MASS.
83-47 West 23rd St., New York City.
Hammond Bldg., 278 Post St.,
San Francisco, Cal.
228 Coristine Building, St. Nicholas St.,
NEG. 283 Montreal, Can.

Base, D3084½. 12 inch, 2 Light, $ 15.00   Butler Silver, $ 16.80
16 inch Seville Shade, No. 269   17.35   Shade,   17.35
                      $ 32.35 $ 34.15

Decoration: Sunset.
Height Overall 22 inches.

Plate 369. Seville shade. Sunset decoration #269. Base #D3084 1/2. 1926.

OLD BRASS, EGYPTIAN BRASS, FLEMISH, ANTIQUE and BRONZE FINISH.
Base D3070½ - 2 Light -------- $13.65   Butler Silver- $15.45
18 inch Seville Shade, No.559 - 20.00   Shade -------- 20.00
                                 $33.65 $35.45
              Decoration : Sevres
Base D3070½ -3 Light ------ $15.00   Butler Silver $16.80
18 inch Seville Shade, No559- 20.00   Shade -------- 20.00
                            $35.00 $36.80
              Decoration Sevres
Neg. #438   Height Over all 24 inches.

Plate 370. Seville shade. Sevres decoration #559. Base #D3070 1/2. No date.

Plate 371. Seville shade. Urn and Flowers decoration #574. Base #D3070 1/2. No date.

OLD BRASS, EGYPTIAN BRASS, FLEMISH, ANTIQUE AND BRONZE FINISH.

THE PAIRPOINT CORPORATION.
NEW BEDFORD, MASS.
43-47 West 23rd St., New York City.
Hammond Bldg., 278 Post St., San Francisco, Cal.
228 Coristine Building, St. Nicholas St., Montreal, Can.
NEG. 440

Base, D3063½. 2 Light,	$15.00	Butler Silver,	$17.35
18 inch Seville Shade. No. 572	22.00	Shade,	22.00
	$37.00		$39.35

Height overall 24 inches.
Decoration; Bird Tapestry.

Base, D3063½. 3 Light,	$16.35	Butler Silver,	$18.65
18 inch Seville Shade. No. 572	22.00	Shade,	22.00
	$38.35		$40.65

Plate 372. Seville shade. Bird Tapestry decoration #572. Base #D3063 1/2. 1926.

OLD BRASS, EGYPTIAN BRASS, FLEMISH, ANTIQUE and BRONZE FINISH.
Base D3067½ - 2 Light $15.00   Butler Silver $ 17.35
18 inch Seville Shade, No. 573 - 20.00   Shade ------   20.00
                               $35.00 $37.35
         Decoration : Coat of Arms.
Base D3067½ - 3 Light $16.35   Butler Silver $ 18.65
18 inch Seville Shade, No. 573 - 20.00   Shade ------   20.00
                               $36.35 $ 38.65
         Decoration :Coat of Arms.
Neg. 441   Height Over all 24½ inches.

Plate 373. Seville shade. Coat of Arms decoration #573. Base #D3067 1/2. No date.

OLD BRASS, EGYPTIAN BRASS, FLEMISH, ANTIQUE AND BRONZE FINISH.

THE PAIRPOINT CORPORATION.
NEW BEDFORD, MASS.
43-47 West 23rd St., New York City.
Hammond Bldg., 278 Post St., San Francisco, Cal.
228 Coristine Building, St. Nicholas St., Montreal, Can.
NEG. 499

Base, D3095½. 2 Light,	$21.00	Butler Silver,	$22.80
16 inch Seville Shade, No. 271,	16.00		16.00
	$37.00		$38.80

Decoration: Urn and Clematis.
Lamps equipped with Alps Green Marble Base.
Height Overall, 22½ inches.

Plate 374. Seville shade. Urn and Clematis decoration #271. Base #D3095 1/2 (Alps green marble). 1926.

BUTLER, EGYPTIAN BRASS, OLD BRASS OR FLEMISH FINISH

THE PAIRPOINT CORPORATION
NEW BEDFORD, MASS.

43-47 West 23rd Street, *New York City*
150 Post Street, Room 300, *San Francisco, Cal.*
225 Coristine Building, St. Nicholas Street
  Montreal, Canada

Neg. 702

Base No. E3051½. 2 Light Electric with No. 11 Finial,
Shade No. X20.   16 inch Seville,
                                       Complete, 27.70
Height overall 25 inches
Brown Scroll Decoration

Plate 375. Seville shade. Brown Scroll decoration #X20. Base #E3051 1/2. 1930.

Plate 376. Seville shade. Stripes and Tulip decoration #558. Base #D3075 1/2. No date.

OLD BRASS, EGYPTIAN BRASS, FLEMISH, ANTIQUE AND BRONZE FINISH.

THE PAIRPOINT CORPORATION.
NEW BEDFORD, MASS.
83-47 West 23rd St., New York City.
Hammond Bldg., 278 Post St.,
San Francisco, Cal.
228 Coristine Building, St. Nicholas St.,

Base, D3075½. 12 inch, 2 Light, $ 14.00   Butler Silver, $ 15.80
14 inch Seville Shade, No. 272   14.00   Shade,   14.00
                              $ 28.00 $ 29.80
Decoration: Raven.
Height Overall 22 inches.

Plate 377. Seville shade. Raven decoration #272. Base #D3075 1/2. 1926.

Plate 378. Seville shade. Blue Parrots decoration #562. Base #D3066 1/2. No date.

Plate 379. Seville shade. *Bird of Paradise* (no #). No base #. No date.

No. C 3062. ELECTROLIER, with 8 Feet Silk Cord. Height of Body, 12 inches.
Plain, One Light, Less Shade, Old Brass Green, Antique or Gun Metal, $12.30   Two Lights, $15.05

THE PAIRPOINT CORPORATION,
NEW BEDFORD, MASS.
38 Murray Street, New York City.
Coristine Building, St. Nicholas St., Montreal, Canada.
717 Market St., San Francisco, Cal.
Neg. 385

No. 1246. 16 inch Springfield Shade, $13.65

TRADE MARK

Plate 380. Springfield shade. *Yellow and pink poppies* decoration #1246. Base #C3062. 1910-1914.

No. C 3034.   ELECTROLIER, with 8 Feet Silk Cord.   Height of Body, 14 inches.
Plain, One Light, Less Shade, Old Brass Green, Antique or Gun Metal @14.00   Two Lights, $16.75

THE PAIRPOINT CORPORATION,
NEW BEDFORD, MASS.
38 Murray Street, New York City.
Coristine Building, St. Nicholas St.,
Montreal, Canada.
717 Market St., San Francisco, Cal.

No. 1255.   16 inch Springfield Shade, $9.10

Plate 381. Springfield shade. *Poppy tapestry* decoration #1255. Base #C3034. 1910-1914.

Plate 382. Springfield shade. *Man in the moon* decoration #1352. Base #3090 (Owl base). 1907.

No. 3088. ELECTROLIER, with 8 Feet Silk Cord, Height of Body, 13 inches.

THE PAIRPOINT CORPORATION,
NEW BEDFORD, MASS.
38 Murray Street, New York City.
36 St. Antoine St., Montreal, Canada.
717 Market St., San Francisco, Cal.
NEG. 395 A

Less Shade, Engraved, Old Brass, - - - - $13.00
" " " Two Lights, 17.00
No. 1356. 16 inch Springfield Shade, $12.00

TRADE MARK

Plate 383. Springfield shade. *Tropical leaves* decoration #1356. Base #3088. 1907.

No. 3092. ELECTROLIER, with 8 Feet Silk Cord, Height of Body, 17 inches.

THE PAIRPOINT CORPORATION,
NEW BEDFORD, MASS.
38 Murray Street, New York City.
36 St. Antoine St., Montreal, Canada.
717 Market St., San Francisco, Cal.
NEG. 400 A

Less Shade, Old Brass, $11.50
" " Two Light, 15.50
No. 1359 — 16 inch Springfield Shade, $24.00
Glass Pendants, $5.00 Extra.

Shade Closed Out.

Copy TRADE MARK

Plate 384. Springfield shade. *Flemish wisteria* decoration #1359 (shown here with prisms). Base #3092 (tree trunk). 1907.

Plate 385. Springfield shade. *Flemish wild rose* decoration #1351. Base #3094. 1907.

Plate 386. Springfield shades. *Flemish maple leaf* decoration #1366; *Gold scroll* decoration #1357; *Butterfly band* decoration #1706. 1907.

No. B 3002. ELECTROLIER, with 8 Feet Silk Cord, Height of Body, 14 inches.

THE PAIRPOINT CORPORATION.
NEW BEDFORD, MASS.
38 Murray Street, New York City.
36 St. Antoine St., Montreal, Canada.
717 Market St., San Francisco, Cal.

Two Lights, 18.00
No. 1379. 16 inch Springfield Shade. 13.00

NEG. 484 A

Plate 387. Springfield shade. *Flemish morning glory* decoration #1379. Base #B3002. 1907.

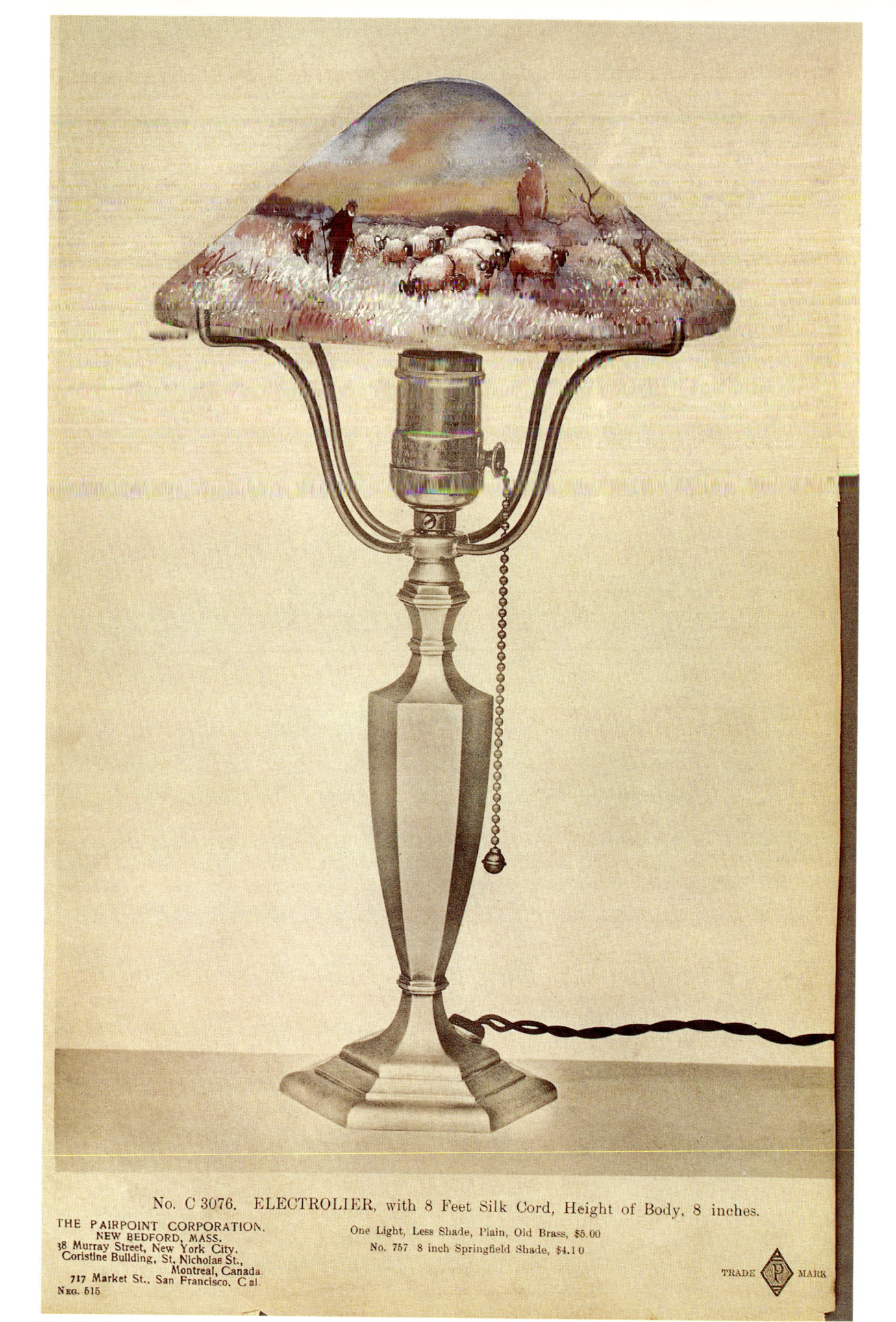

No. C 3076. ELECTROLIER, with 8 Feet Silk Cord, Height of Body, 8 inches.

THE PAIRPOINT CORPORATION,
NEW BEDFORD, MASS.
38 Murray Street, New York City.
Coristine Building, St. Nicholas St.,
Montreal, Canada.
717 Market St., San Francisco, Cal.
NEG. 515

One Light, Less Shade, Plain, Old Brass, $5.00
No. 757 8 inch Springfield Shade, $4.10

TRADE MARK

Plate 388. Springfield shade. *Shepherd and his flock* decoration #757. Base #C3076. 1910-1914.

No. B 3021. ELECTROLIER, with 8 Feet Silk Cord, Height of Body, 6½ inches.

THE PAIRPOINT CORPORATION,
NEW BEDFORD, MASS.
38 Murray Street, New York City.
Coristine Building, St. Nicholas St.,
Montreal, Canada.
717 Market St., San Francisco, Cal.
NEG. 517

One Light, Less Shade, Plain, Old Brass, $5.50
No. 756. 8 inch Springfield Shade, $4.55

TRADE MARK

Plate 389. Springfield shade. *Laurel leaf with border* decoration #756. Base #B3021. 1910-1914.

No. B 3021. ELECTROLIER, with 8 Feet Silk Cord, Height of Body, 6½ inches.

THE PAIRPOINT CORPORATION.
NEW BEDFORD, MASS.
38 Murray Street, New York City.
36 St. Antoine St., Montreal, Canada.
717 Market St., San Francisco, Cal.
NEG. 519 A

Less Shade. Plain, Old Brass, $5.50
    "   Engraved, "   6.00
No. 1382. 8 inch Springfield Shade, $2.00

TRADE MARK

Plate 390. Springfield shade. *Parasol* decoration #1382. Base #B3021. 1907.

No. 3052½ ELECTROLIER, with 8 Feet Silk Cord, Height of Body, 11¼ inches.

THE PAIRPOINT CORPORATION,
NEW BEDFORD, MASS.
38 Murray Street, New York City.
36 St. Antoine St., Montreal, Canada.
717 Market St., San Francisco, Cal.
NEG. 533 A

Less Shade, Old Brass, Green, Engraved. $15.00
Two Lights, 10.00
No. 999. 16 inch Springfield Shade, 10.00

Plate 391. Springfield shade. *Rhododendrons* decoration #999. Base #3052 1/2. 1907.

No. 3035. ELECTROLIER, with 8 Feet Silk Cord, Height of Body, 12½ inches.

THE PAIRPOINT CORPORATION.
NEW BEDFORD, MASS.
38 Murray Street, New York City.
36 St. Antoine St., Montreal, Canada.
717 Market St., San Francisco, Cal.

NEG. 536 A

Less Shade, Old Brass, $13.00
" " Two Lights, 17.00
No. 994. **16** inch Springfield Shade, 10.00

Plate 392. Springfield shade. *Clematis* **decoration #994. Base #3035. 1907.**

No. B 3067. ELECTROLIER. With 8 Feet Silk Cord, Height of Body, 13 inches.
Special Two Light Fixture, Less Shade, Old Brass Green, Antique or Gun Metal, $10.00

THE PAIRPOINT CORPORATION,
NEW BEDFORD, MASS.
38 Murray Street, New York City.
Coristine Building, St. Nicholas St.,
Montreal, Canada.
717 Market St., San Francisco, Cal.
NEG. 545

No. 736. 16 inch Springfield Shade, $11.40

TRADE MARK

Plate 393. Springfield shade. *Wedgewood band* decoration #736. Base #B3067. 1910-1914.

No. C 3078. ELECTROLIER. With 8 Feet Silk Cord, Height of Body, 13½ inches.
Special Two Light Fixture, Less Shade, Plain Old Brass Green, Antique or Gun Metal, $10.00

THE PAIRPOINT CORPORATION,
NEW BEDFORD, MASS.
38 Murray Street, New York City.
Coristine Building, St. Nicholas St.,
Montreal, Canada.
717 Market St., San Francisco, Cal.
NEG. 562

No. 735. 16 inch Springfield Shade, $9.55

TRADE MARK

Plate 394. Springfield shade. *Urn with swag* decoration #735. Base #C3078. 1910-1914.

Plate 395. Springfield shade. *Jasper urn* decoration #734. Base #C3015. 1910-1914.

No. C 3067/739. ELECTROLIER. With 8 Feet Silk Cord, Height of Body, 12½ inches. Complete, $2
Lamp Base, Less Shade, with Special Two Light Fixture, Old Brass Trimmings, $12.30

THE PAIRPOINT CORPORATION,
NEW BEDFORD, MASS.
38 Murray Street, New York City.
Coristine Building, St. Nicholas St.,
Montreal, Canada.
717 Market St., San Francisco, Cal.
NEG. 565

No. 739 16 inch Springfield Shade, $7.75

TRADE

Plate 396. Springfield shade. *Floral with heart band* decoration #739. Base #C3067/739 (matching glass base). 1910-1914.

No. C 3067/738. ELECTROLIER. With 8 Feet Silk Cord, Height of Body, 12½ inches. Complete, $2

Lamp Base, Less Shade, with Special Two Light Fixture, Old Brass Trimmings, $14.55

THE PAIRPOINT CORPORATION,
NEW BEDFORD, MASS.
38 Murray Street, New York City.
Coristine Building, St. Nicholas St.,
Montreal, Canada.
717 Market St., San Francisco, Cal.
Neg. 571

No. 738 16 inch Springfield Shade, $13.65

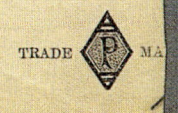

TRADE MA

Plate 397. Springfield shade. *Cherubs in medallions with jasper background* decoration #738. Base #C3067/738 (matching glass base). 1910-1914.

No. B 3094.   ELECTROLIER.   With 8 Feet Silk Cord, Height of Body, 12 inches.

Special Two Light Fixture, Less Shade, Plain Old Brass Green, Antique or Gun Metal, $9.00

THE PAIRPOINT CORPORATION,
NEW BEDFORD, MASS.
38 Murray Street, New York City.
Coristine Building, St. Nicholas St.,
Montreal, Canada.
717 Market St., San Francisco, Cal.
NEG. 578

No. 737.   16 inch Springfield Shade, $7.75

TRADE MARK

Plate 398. Springfield shade. *Venetian boats at sea* decoration #737. Base #B3094. 1910-1914.

No. 3085.   ELECTROLIER, with 8 Feet Silk Cord, Height of Body, 14 inches.

THE PAIRPOINT CORPORATION.
NEW BEDFORD, MASS.
38 Murray Street, New York City.
485 St. Catherine St., Montreal, Canada.
717 Market St., San Francisco, Cal.
NEG 735 A

Less Shade, Engraved, Old Brass, $9.50
  "   "   "   Two Lights, 13.50
No. 1357.   16-inch Springfield Shade, $10.00

TRADE MARK

COPY

Plate 399. Springfield shade. *Floral scroll* decoration #1357. Base #3085. 1907–1910.

No. C 3098. ELECTROLIER. With 8 Feet Silk Cord, Height of Body, 12 inches.

THE PAIRPOINT CORPORATION, Lamp Base, Less Shade, with Special Two Light Fixture, Old Brass, Green or Bronze, $10.95
NEW BEDFORD, MASS.
43-47 West 23rd St., New York City.　　　　No. 876. 16 inch Springfield Shade, Jonquil Decoration, $10.95
402 Columbus Memorial Bldg., Chicago.
140 Geary St., San Francisco, Cal.
Coristine Building, St. Nicholas St.,
Neg. 890　　　Montreal, Canada.

Plate 400. Springfield shade. Jonquil decoration #876. Base #C3098. 1915.

No. 3085.   ELECTROLIER, with 8 Feet Silk Cord, Height of Body, 14 inches.

THE PAIRPOINT CORPORATION.
NEW BEDFORD, MASS.
38 Murray Street, New York City.
485 St. Catherine St., Montreal, Canada.
717 Market St., San Francisco, Cal.
NEG 735 A

Less Shade, Engraved, Old Brass, $9.50
"   "   "   "   Two Lights, 13.50
No. 1357. 16-inch Springfield Shade, $10.00

TRADE MARK.

COPY

Plate 399. Springfield shade. *Floral scroll* decoration #1357. Base #3085. 1907-1910.

No. C 3098. ELECTROLIER. With 8 Feet Silk Cord, Height of Body, 12 inches.

THE PAIRPOINT CORPORATION, Lamp Base, Less Shade, with Special Two Light Fixture, Old Brass, Green or Bronze, $10.95
NEW BEDFORD, MASS.
43-47 West 23rd St., New York City. No. 876. 16 inch Springfield Shade, Jonquil Decoration, $10.95
402 Columbus Memorial Bldg., Chicago.
140 Geary St., San Francisco, Cal.
Coristine Building, St. Nicholas St.,
Neg. 890   Montreal, Canada.

Plate 400. Springfield shade. Jonquil decoration #876. Base #C3098. 1915.

No. C 3084.　ELECTROLIER.　With 8 Feet Silk Cord, Height of Body, 12½ inches.

THE PAIRPOINT CORPORATION,
NEW BEDFORD, MASS.
43-47 West 23rd St., New York City.
402 Columbus Memorial Bldg., Chicago.
140 Geary St., San Francisco, Cal.
Coristine Building, St. Nicholas St.,
NEG. 891　　Montreal, Canada.

Lamp Base, Less Shade, with Special Two Light Fixture, Mahogany with Brass Trimmings, $8.65
No. 874.　16 inch Springfield Shade (Autumn Decoration,) $11.85

Plate 401. Springfield shade. Autumn decoration #874. Base #C3084. 1915.

No. C 3099/875.   ELECTROLIER.   Wired with 8 Feet Silk Cord.

THE PAIRPOINT CORPORATION, NEW BEDFORD, MASS.
43-47 West 23rd St., New York City.
402 Columbus Memorial Bldg., Chicago.
140 Geary St., San Francisco, Cal.
Coristine Building, St. Nicholas St., Montreal, Canada
Neg 1028

(Height of Body, 12¾ inches. Height to Top of Shade, 21¾ inches.)
No. C 3099. Base, Less Shade, Two Light,
Mahogany Sub Base with Gun Metal Trimmings, $11.85
No. 875. 16 inch Springfield Shade, 10.95
Complete, $22.80

TRADE MARK

Plate 402. Springfield shade. *Berry and leaf* decoration #875. Base #C3099/875 (matching glass base). 1915.

No. 3084. ELECTROLIER, with 8 Feet Silk Cord, Height of Body, 12 inches.

THE PAIRPOINT CORPORATION,
NEW BEDFORD, MASS.
38 Murray Street, New York City.
36 St. Antoine St., Montreal, Canada.
717 Market St., San Francisco, Cal.
NEG. 391 A

Less Shade, Engraved, Old Brass, $13.00
" Plain, " 11.00
Two Light, $4.00 Extra.
No. 1350, Inch Shade, $20.00

TRADE MARK.

Plate 403. Springfield shade. *Lily* decoration #1350. Base #3084. 1907.

No. B 3021. ELECTROLIER, with 8 Feet Silk Cord, Height of Body, 6½ inches.

THE PAIRPOINT CORPORATION,
NEW BEDFORD, MASS.
38 Murray Street, New York City.
485 St. Catherine St., Montreal, Canada.
717 Market St., San Francisco, Cal.
Neg. 659 A

Less Shade, Plain, Old Brass, $5.50
" Engraved, " 6.00
No. 940. 8 inch Stratford Shade, $7.00

TRADE MARK

Plate 404. Stratford shade. Puffy. *Floral on green background* **decoration #940 (close top). Base #B3021. 1907-1910.**

No. B 3048.   ELECTROLIER, with 8 Feet Silk Cord, Height of Body, 6½ inches.

THE PAIRPOINT CORPORATION,
NEW BEDFORD, MASS.
38 Murray Street, New York City.
485 St. Catherine St., Montreal, Canada.
717 Market St., San Francisco, Cal.
NEG. 649 A

No. 3048. Less Shade, Old Brass, $6.50
No. 938. 8 inch Stratford, $7.00

Plate 405.   Stratford shade. Puffy. *Floral, pink on old rose background* decoration #938 (close top). Base #B3048. 1907-1910.

BUTLER, EGYPTIAN BRASS, OLD BRASS OR FLEMISH FINISH

THE PAIRPOINT CORPORATION
NEW BEDFORD, MASS.

43-47 West 23rd Street, New York City
150 Post Street, Room 300, San Francisco, Cal.
228 Coristine Building, St. Nicholas Street
Montreal, Canada

Neg. 704

Base No. E3056. 2-Light Electric,
Shade No. X25. 14 inch Stratford,
Complete,
Height overall 22 inches
Hollyhocks Decoration

19.70
13.20
32.90

Plate 406. Stratford shade. Puffy. Hollyhocks decoration #X25 (open top). Base #E3056. 1930.

THE PAIRPOINT CORPORATION
NEW BEDFORD, MASS.
43-47 West 22nd Street, New York City
150 Post Street, Room 100, San Francisco, Cal.

BUTLER, EGYPTIAN BRASS, OLD BRASS OR FLEMISH FINISH

Base No. E3063.
Shade No. X24.
1-Light Electric,
8 inch Stratford,
Complete
Height overall 14 inches

Base No. E3064.
Shade No. 438.
1-Light Electric,
8 inch Stratford,
Complete
Height overall 13¾ inches
Wild Rose Decoration

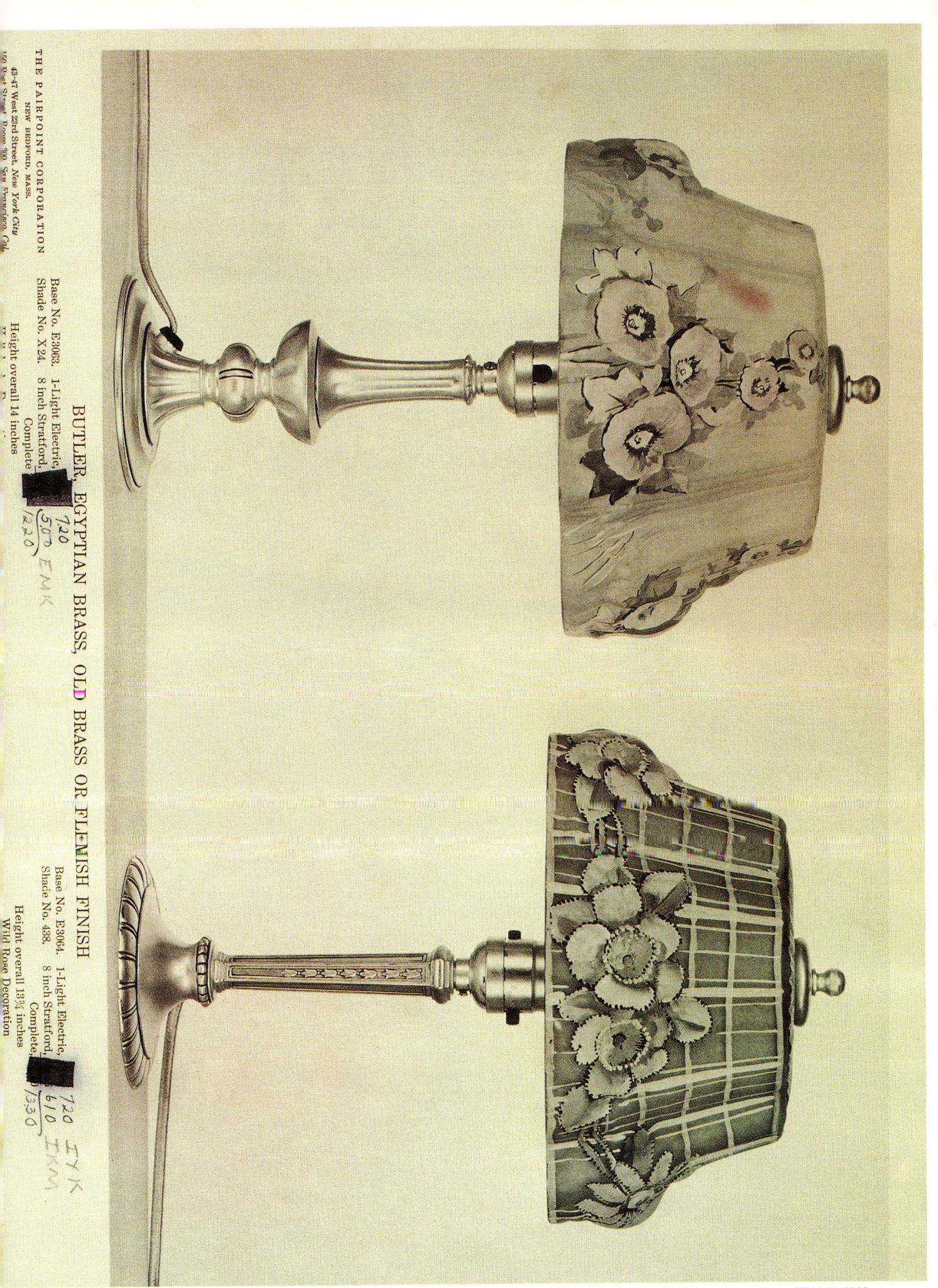

Plate 407. Stratford shades. Puffy. Hollyhocks decoration #X24 (open top). Base #E3063; Wild Rose decoration #438 (open top). Base #E3064. 1930.

BUTLER, EGYPTIAN BRASS, OLD BRASS OR FLEMISH FINISH

Base E305.	1 Light Electric,
Shade No. X11.	8 inch Stratford,
	Complete,

Height overall 15 inches

- X10. 8 inch Stratford "Nasturtium" decoration.
- X11. 8 inch Stratford "Chrysanthemum" decoration.
- X12. 8 inch Stratford "Tulip" decoration.
- X17. 8 inch Rose "Petunia" decoration.

Lamp and Shade complete in lots of 12, with assorted shades in any of the following decorations.

Base E3054.	1 Light Electric,
Shade No. X10.	8 inch Stratford,
	Complete,

THE PAIRPOINT CORPORATION
NEW BEDFORD, MASS.
43-47 West 23rd Street, - NewYork City
130 Post Street, Room 300, San Francisco, Cal.
222½ Coristine Building, - Montreal, Canada
Neg. 722 - St. Nicholas Street

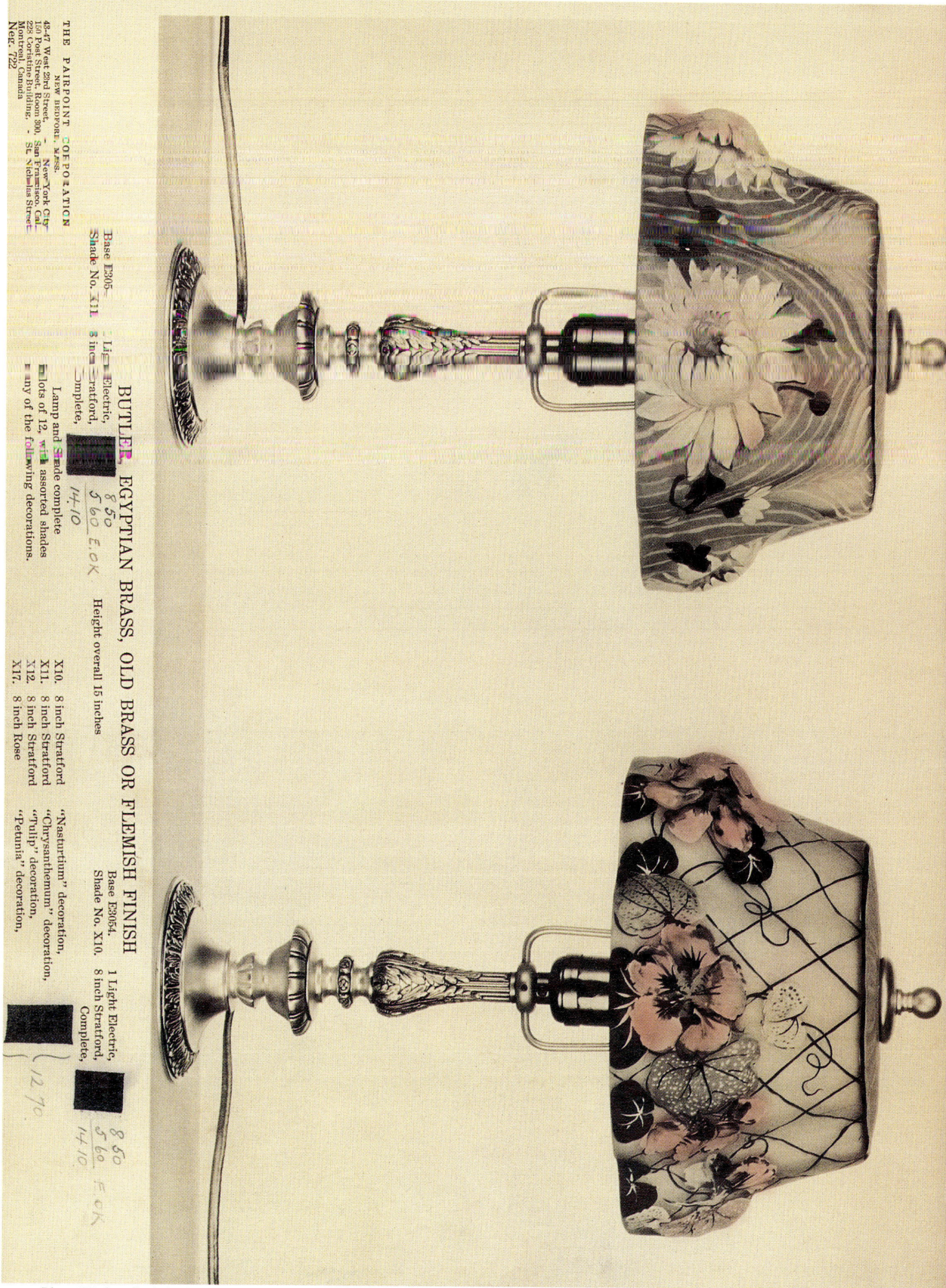

Plate 408. Stratford shades. Puffy. Chrysanthemum decoration #X11 (open top). Base #E3054; Nasturtium decoration #X10 (open top). Base #E3054. 1930.

THE
PAIRPOINT CORPORATION
NEW BEDFORD, MASS.
43-47 West 23rd Street, — New York City
150 Post Street Room 30 San Francisco, Cal.

BUTLER EGYPTIAN BRASS, OLD BRASS OR FLEMISH FINISH

Base E3054. 1 Light Electric,
Shade No. X12. 8 inch Stratford,
Complete,

Lamp and Shade complete
in lots of 12, with assorted shades

X10. 8 inch Stratford "Nasturtium" decoration,
X12. 8 inch Stratford "Chrysanthemum" decoration,

Height overall 15 inches

Base E3054. 1 Light Electric,
Shade No. X17. 8 inch Rose,
Complete,

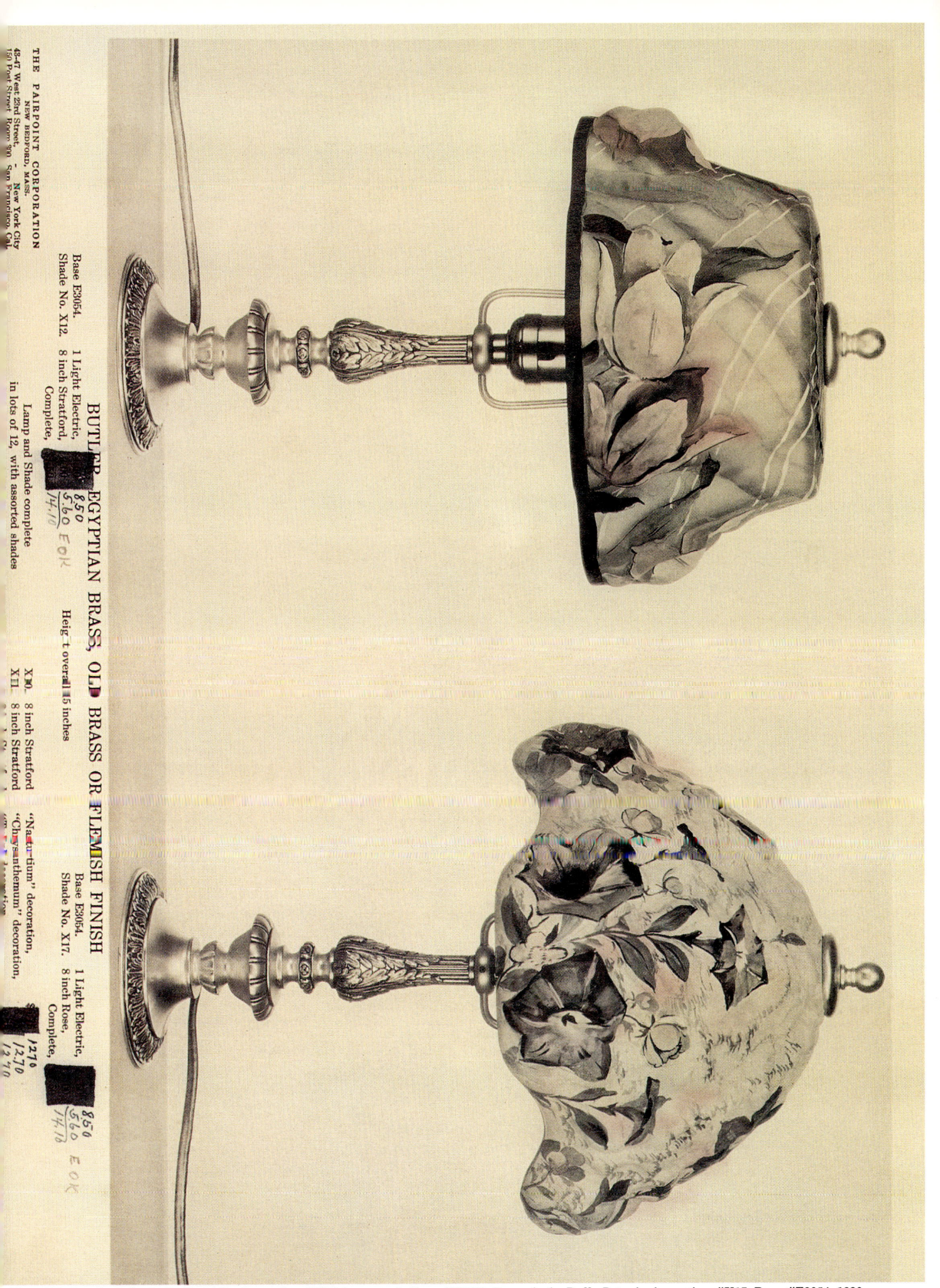

Plate 409. Stratford shade. Puffy. Tulip decoration #X12 (open top). Base #E3054; Rose shade. Puffy. Petunia decoration #X17. Base #E3054. 1930.

BUTLER, EGYPTIAN BRASS, OLD BRASS OR FLEMISH FINISH

Base E3056. 2 Light Electric,
Shade No. X15. 14 inch Stratford,
Complete,
Decoration: "Chrysanthemum"
Height overall, 22 inches

THE PAIRPOINT CORPORATION
NEW BEDFORD, MASS.

43-47 West 23rd Street, - New York City
150 Post Street, Room 300, San Francisco, Cal.
228 Coristine Building, - St. Nicholas Street
Montreal, Canada
Neg. 740

Plate 410. Stratford shade. Puffy. Chrysanthemum decoration #X15 (open top). Base #E3056. 1930.

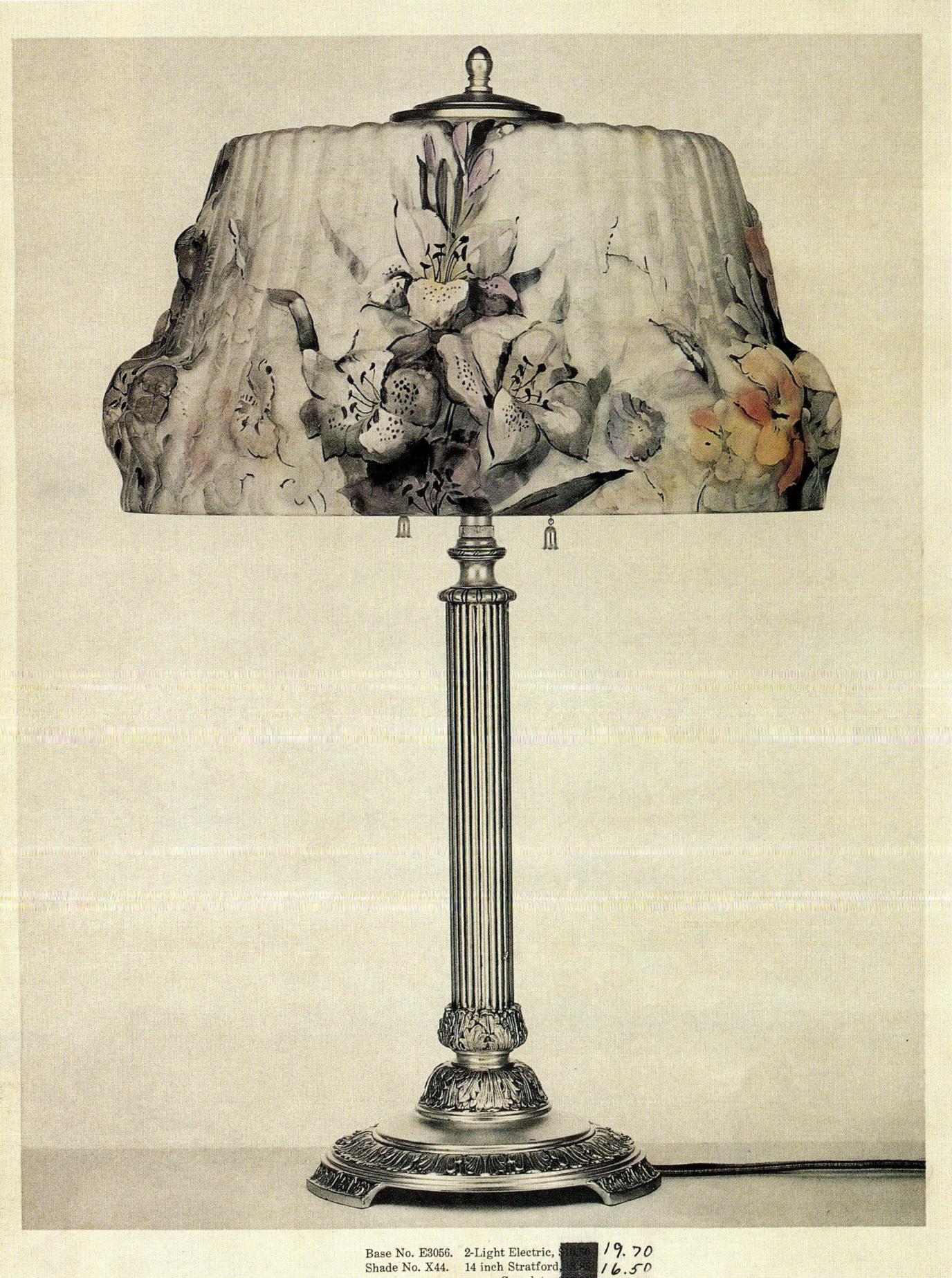

Base No. E3056. 2-Light Electric, ~~$36.50~~ 19.70
Shade No. X44. 14 inch Stratford, ~~$35.00~~ 16.50
Complete, ~~$99.00~~ 36.20
Height overall 22 inches
"Gladioli" Decoration
BUTLER SILVER OR EGYPTIAN BRASS FINISH

THE PAIRPOINT CORPORATION
NEW BEDFORD, MASS.

43-47 West 23rd Street, *New York City*
150 Post Street, *San Francisco, Cal.*
228 Coristine Building, St. Nicholas Street
Montreal, Canada
Neg. 730

Plate 411. Stratford shade. Puffy. Gladioli decoration #X44 (open top). Base #E3056. 1930.

Plate 412. Stratford shade. Puffy. *Hummingbird and roses* decoration (no #) (open top). No base #. No date.

Plate 413. Tisbury shade. Engraved crystal. *Fount and shade (Astral lamp, with crystal prisms) (no #). Base #E3083 (white marble). 1930.*

No. B 3093. ELECTROLIER. With 8 Feet Silk Cord, Height of Body, 12 inches.

THE PAIRPOINT CORPORATION,
NEW BEDFORD, MASS.
38 Murray Street, New York City.
Coristine Building, St. Nicholas St.,
Montreal, Canada.
717 Market St., San Francisco, Cal.
NEG 58

One Light, Less Shade. Old Brass Green, Antique or Gun Metal, $13.50
Two   "   "   "   "   "   "   "   17.50
No. 804. 14 inch Tivoli Shade, $15.00

Plate 414. Tivoli shade. Ribbed. *Rose tapestry* decoration #804. Base #B3093 (glass column insert). 1910-1914.

No. C 3003.   ELECTROLIER.   With 8 Feet Silk Cord, Height of Body, 15 inches.

THE PAIRPOINT CORPORATION,
NEW BEDFORD, MASS.
38 Murray Street, New York City.
Coristine Building, St. Nicholas St.,
Montreal, Canada.
717 Market St., San Francisco, Cal.

One Light, Less Shade, Old Brass, Antique Green or Gun Metal, $15.50
Two Light,   "   "   "   "   "   "   "   "   19.50

No. 807. 14 inch Tivoli Shade, $16.00

NEG 71

TRADE

Plate 415. Tivoli shade. Ribbed. *Rose lattice* decoration #807. Base #C3003 (glass column insert). 1910-1914.

No. B 3098. ELECTROLIER. With 8 Feet Silk Cord, Height of Body, 13 inches.

One Light, Less Shade, Old Brass Green, Antique, or Gun Metal, $14.00 Two Light, $18.00
No. 808. 14 inch Tivoli Shade, $15.00

THE PAIRPOINT CORPORATION,
NEW BEDFORD, MASS.
38 Murray Street, New York City.
Coristine Building, St. Nicholas St.,
Montreal, Canada.
717 Market St., San Francisco, Cal.
NEG. 85

TRADE P MARK

Plate 416. Tivoli shade. Ribbed. *Fleur-de-lys with rose border* **decoration #808. Base #B3098. 1910-1914.**

No. B 3096. ELECTROLIER. With 8 Feet Silk Cord, Height of Body, 12 inches.

THE PAIRPOINT CORPORATION,
NEW BEDFORD, MASS.
38 Murray Street, New York City.
Coristine Building, St. Nicholas St.,
Montreal, Canada.
717 Market St., San Francisco, Cal.

One Light, Less Shade, Old Brass Green, Antique, or Gun Metal, $13.50
Two Light, $17.50
No. 814. 14 inch Tivoli Shade, $17.00

TRADE MARK

NEG 92

Plate 417. Tivoli shade. Ribbed. *Floral with scroll border* decoration #814. Base #B3096. 1910-1914.

No. B 3099. ELECTROLIER. With 8 Feet Silk Cord, Height of Body, 14 inches.

THE PAIRPOINT CORPORATION,
NEW BEDFORD, MASS.
38 Murray Street, New York City.
Coristine Building, St. Nicholas St.,
Montreal, Canada.
717 Market St., San Francisco, Cal.
NEG. 93

One Light, Less Shade, Old Brass Green. Antique or Gun Metal, $14.50
Two Light, $18.50
No. 805. 14 inch Tivoli Shade, $14.00

TRADE MARK

Plate 418. Tivoli shade. Ribbed. *Peonies with scroll border* decoration #805. Base #B3099. 1910-1914.

Plate 419. Tivoli shade. Ribbed. *White Poppy tapestry with gold border* decoration #404. Base #C3020. 1910-1914.

No. C 3021. ELECTROLIER, with 8 Feet Silk Cord. Height of Body, 13 inches.

Plain, One Light, Less Shade. Old Brass Antique or Gun Metal, $16.00 Two Lights, $18.75
Engraved, " " " " " " " " " 18.00 " " 20.75
Plain Silver, $17.50 " " 20.25
Eng. " 19.50 " " 22.25

Fancy Coloring, $1.00 extra.

THE PAIRPOINT CORPORATION,
NEW BEDFORD, MASS.
38 Murray Street, New York City,
Coristine Building, St. Nicholas St.,
Montreal, Canada.
717 Market St., San Francisco, Cal.

No. 516 14 inch Tivoli Shade, $13.00

NEG. 234

TRADE P MARK

Plate 420. Tivoli shade. Ribbed. *Gristmill* decoration #516. Base #C3021. 1910-1914.

No. C 3013. ELECTROLIER, with 8 Feet Silk Cord. Height of Body, 14 inches.

One Light, Less Shade, Old Brass Green, Antique or Gun Metal, $14.00   Two Lights, $16.75

THE PAIRPOINT CORPORATION,
NEW BEDFORD, MASS.
38 Murray Street, New York City.
Coristine Building, St. Nicholas St.,
Montreal, Canada.
717 Market St., San Francisco, Cal.

No. 515   14 inch Tivoli Shade, $13.00

Plate 421. Tivoli shade. Ribbed. *Evening lighthouse* decoration #515. Base #C3013. 1910–1914.

No. C 3022. ELECTROLIER, with 8 Feet Silk Cord. Height of Body, 9½ inches.

Plain, One Light, Less Shade, Old Brass, Antique or Gun Metal, $10.50
Engraved, "   "   "   "   "   "   "   "   "   "   12.00

THE PAIRPOINT CORPORATION,
NEW BEDFORD, MASS.
38 Murray Street, New York City.
Coristine Building, St. Nicholas St.,
Montreal, Canada.
717 Market St., San Francisco, Cal.
NEG. 249

Plain Silver, $11.50
Engraved Silver,   13.00
Fancy Coloring, $1.00 extra.
No. 1306. 8 inch Tivoli Shade, $6.00

TRADE MARK

Plate 422. Tivoli shade. Ribbed. *Violets with stripes* decoration #1306. Base #C3022. 1910-1914.

No. C 3024.   ELECTROLIER, with 8 Feet Silk Cord.   Height of Body, 7½ inches.

Plain.   One Light, Less Shade, Old Brass, Antique or Gun Metal, $7.00
Engraved,   "   "   "   "   "   "   "   "   "   8.00

Plain Silver, $7.50
Engraved Silver,   8.50
Fancy Coloring, $1.00 extra.

THE PAIRPOINT CORPORATION,
NEW BEDFORD, MASS.
38 Murray Street, New York City.
Coristine Building, St. Nicholas St.,
Montreal, Canada.
717 Market St., San Francisco, Cal.
NEG. 252

No. 1310.   8 inch Tivoli Shade, $6.00

Plate 423. Tivoli shade. Ribbed. *Floral lattice* decoration #1310. Base #C3024. 1910-1914.

No. C 3026. ELECTROLIER, with 8 Feet Silk Cord. Height of Body, 7½ inches.

Plain, One Light, Less Shade, Old Brass, Antique or Gun Metal, $7.00
Engraved, " " " " " " " " " 8.00

THE PAIRPOINT CORPORATION,
NEW BEDFORD, MASS.
38 Murray Street, New York City.
Coristine Building, St. Nicholas St.,
Montreal, Canada.
717 Market St., San Francisco, Cal.
NEG. 250

Plain Silver, $7.50
Engraved Silver, 8.50
Fancy Coloring, $1.00 extra.
No. 1305. 8 inch Tivoli Shade, $7.00

Plate 424. Tivoli shade. Ribbed. *Floral swag and stripe* decoration #1305. Base #C3026. 1910-1914.

No. C 3025. ELECTROLIER, with 8 Feet Silk Cord. Height of Body, 7½ inches

Plain. One Light, Less Shade, Old Brass, Antique or Gun Metal, $7.00
Engraved, "   "   "   "   "   "   "   "   "   "   8.00

THE PAIRPOINT CORPORATION,
NEW BEDFORD, MASS.
38 Murray Street, New York City.
Coristine Building, St. Nicholas St.,
Montreal, Canada.
717 Market St., San Francisco, Cal.

Plain Silver, $7.50
Engraved Silver, 8.50
Fancy Coloring, $1.00 extra.
No. 402. 8 inch Tivoli Shade, $7.00

Plate 425. Tivoli shade. Ribbed. *Cameo border* decoration #402. Base #C3025. 1910-1914.

No. B 3021.   ELECTROLIER, with 8 Feet Silk Cord.   Height of Body, 6½ inches.

THE PAIRPOINT CORPORATION,
NEW BEDFORD, MASS.
38 Murray Street, New York City.
Coristine Building, St. Nicholas St.,
Montreal, Canada.
717 Market St., San Francisco, Cal.
NEG 261

Plain.   Less Shade, Old Brass, Antique or Gun Metal, $5.50
Engraved,   "   "   "   "   "   "   "   "   6.00

No. 1316   8 inch Tivoli Shade, $5.00

TRADE MARK

Plate 426. Tivoli shade. Ribbed. *Floral bouquet with ribbon and border* decoration #1316. Base #B3021. 1910-1914.

No. 30934. ELECTROLIER, with 8 Feet Silk Cord. Height of Body, 18 inches.
One Light, Less Shade, Old Brass Green, Antique or Gun Metal, $8.50   Two Lights, $11.25
No. 800   14 inch Tivoli Shade, $10.00

THE PAIRPOINT CORPORATION,
NEW BEDFORD, MASS.
38 Murray Street, New York City.
Coristine Building, St. Nicholas St.,
Montreal, Canada.
717 Market St., San Francisco, Cal.
NEG 278

Plate 427. Tivoli shade. Ribbed. *Tulips and poppies* decoration #800. Base #3093 1/2. 1910-1914.

No. C 3015.   ELECTROLIER, with 8 Feet Silk Cord.   Height of Body, 14½ inches.
One Light, Less Shade, Old Brass Green, Antique or Gun Metal, $13.00   Two Lights, $15.75

THE PAIRPOINT CORPORATION,
NEW BEDFORD, MASS.
38 Murray Street, New York City.
Coristine Building, St. Nicholas St.,
Montreal, Canada.
717 Market St., San Francisco, Cal.
Neg 280

No. 801. 14 inch Tivoli Shade, $10.00

TRADE ⟨P⟩ M.

Plate 428. Tivoli shade. Ribbed. *Oriental poppies* **decoration #801. Base #C3015. 1910-1914.**

No. C 3015   ELECTROLIER, with 8 Feet Silk Cord, Height of Body, 14½ inches.
Special Two Light Fixture, Less Shade, Old Brass Green, Antique or Gun Metal, $13.00

THE PAIRPOINT CORPORATION,
NEW BEDFORD, MASS.
38 Murray Street, New York City.
Coristine Building, St. Nicholas St.,
Montreal, Canada.
717 Market St., San Francisco, Cal.

No. 651. 14 inch Tivoli Shade, $8.20

Plate 429. Tivoli shade. Ribbed. *Hydrangeas and ribbon* decoration #651. Base #C3015. 1910-1914.

No. C 3051. ELECTROLIER, with 8 Feet Silk Cord, Height of Body, 9 inches.

Plain. One Light, Less Shade, Old Brass, Antique or Gun Metal, $10.00
Engraved, " " " " " " Green " " " 12.30
" " " " " French Grey, $10.95
" " " " Engraved, French Gray, 13.20
Fancy Coloring, $ .95 Extra.

No. 652. 8 inch Tivoli Shade, $4.10

THE PAIRPOINT CORPORATION,
NEW BEDFORD, MASS.
38 Murray Street, New York City.
Coristine Building, St. Nicholas St.,
Montreal, Canada.
717 Market St., San Francisco, Cal.

Plate 430. Tivoli shade. Ribbed. *Sweet pea* decoration #652. Base #C3051. 1910-1914.

No. C 3068/744. ELECTROLIER, with 8 Feet Silk Cord, Height of Body, 11 inches, Complete, $22.30

THE PAIRPOINT CORPORATION, NEW BEDFORD, MASS.
38 Murray Street, New York City.
Coristine Building, St. Nicholas St., Montreal, Canada.
717 Market St., San Francisco, Cal.
NEG. 549

Lamp Base with Special Two Light Fixture, Old Brass Trimmings, $13.20
No. 744. 14 inch Tivoli Shade, $9.10

TRADE P MARK.

Plate 431. Tivoli shade. Ribbed. *Pink daisies* decoration #744. Base #C3068/744 (matching glass base). 1910-1914.

No. C 3077. ELECTROLIER, with 8 Feet Silk Cord, Height of Body, 9 inches.

THE PAIRPOINT CORPORATION,
NEW BEDFORD, MASS.
38 Murray Street, New York City.
Coristine Building, St. Nicholas St.,
Montreal, Canada
717 Market St., San Francisco, Cal.

Neg. 522

One Light, Less Shade, Engraved, Old Brass Green, $5.95
No. 753. 8 inch Tivoli Shade, $4.55

TRADE MARK

Plate 432. Tivoli shade. Ribbed. *Farm scene* decoration #753. Base #C3077. 1910-1914.

No. C 3067 745. ELECTROLIER. With 8 Feet Silk Cord, Height of Body, 12¼ Inches. Complete, $21.10
Lamp Base, Less Shade, with Special Two Light Fixture, Old Brass Trimmings, $12.75

THE PAIRPOINT CORPORATION,
NEW BEDFORD, MASS.
38 Murray Street, New York City.
Coristine Building, St. Nicholas St.,
Montreal, Canada.
717 Market St., San Francisco, Cal.
NEG. 576

No. 745. 14 inch Tivoli Shade, $9.10

TRADE P MARK

Plate 433. Tivoli shade. Ribbed. *White rose* decoration #745. Base #C3067/745 (matching glass base). No date.

No. C 3069/732. ELECTROLIER. With 8 Feet Silk Cord, Height of Body, 16½ inches. Complete, $24.5...

Lamp Base, Less Shade, with Special Two Light Fixture, Old Brass Trimmings, $13.65

THE PAIRPOINT CORPORATION,
NEW BEDFORD, MASS.
38 Murray Street, New York City.
Coristine Building, St. Nicholas St.,
Montreal, Canada.
717 Market Street, San Francisco, Cal.
NEG. 583

No. 732. 14 inch Tivoli Shade, $10.90

TRADE P MARK

Plate 434. Tivoli shade. Ribbed. *Bearded iris* decoration #732. Base #C3069/732 (matching glass base). No date.

NEG 787 A

No. B 3056. ELECTROLIER, with 8 Feet Silk Cord, Height of Body, 14½ inches.

THE PAIRPOINT CORPORATION.
NEW BEDFORD, MASS.
38 Murray Street, New York City.
485 St. Catherine St., Montreal, Canada.
717 Market St., San Francisco, Cal.

Less Shade, Old Brass, Antique Green, Gun Metal or Copper, $19.50
Fancy Inlaid, $21.50
Two Lights, $4.00 extra.
No. 540. 16 inch Torino Shade. $20.00

Plate 435. Torino shade. *Colonial couple* decoration #540 . Base #B3056. 1907-1910.

Plate 436. Torino shade. *Floral bouquet* decoration #968. Base #B3055 1/2. No date.

No. B 3056. ELECTROLIER, with 8 Feet Silk Cord. Height of Body, 14½ Inches.
One Light, Less Shade, Old Brass Green, Gun Metal or Antique, $19.50   Two Lights, $23.50
Fancy Coloring, $2.00 extra.

THE PAIRPOINT CORPORATION,
NEW BEDFORD, MASS.
38 Murray Street, New York City.
Coristine Building, St. Nicholas St.,
Montreal, Canada.
717 Market St., San Francisco, Cal.

No. 1716   16 inch Torino Shade, $12.00

NEG. 964 A

TRADE P MARK

Plate 437. Torino shade. *English cottage* decoration #1716. Base #B3056. 1910-1914.

No. D 3000 872. ELECTROLIER. With 8 Feet Silk Cord, Complete, $29.10

THE PAIRPOINT CORPORATION,
NEW BEDFORD, MASS.

43-47 West 23rd St., New York City.
402 Columbus Memorial Bldg., Chicago.
140 Geary St., San Francisco, Cal.
Coristine Building, St. Nicholas St.,
NEG. 872   Montreal, Canada.

Height of Body, 18¼ inches   Height to Top of Shade, 26¼ inches.
No. D 3000 Lamp Base, Less Shade, with Special Three Light Fixture, Mahogany Base.
Gun Metal Trimmings. $13.20
No. 872—18 inch Touraine Shade (Decoration, Green Leather effect), $15.90

TRADE MA

Plate 438. Touraine shade. Green leather effect decoration #872. Base #D3000/872 (matching glass base). 1915.

No. D 3000/873.   ELECTROLIER.   With 8 Feet Silk Cord, Complete, $33.65

THE PAIRPOINT CORPORATION,
NEW BEDFORD, MASS.
43-47 West 23rd St., New York City.
402 Columbus Memorial Bldg., Chicago.
140 Geary St., San Francisco, Cal.
Coristine Building, St. Nicholas St.,
Montreal, Canada.
NEG. 873

Height of Body, 16½ inches.   Height to Top of Shade, 26½ inches
No. D 3000 Lamp Base. Less Shade, with Special Three Light Fixture, Mahogany Base,
Gun Metal Trimmings, $13.65
No. 873   18 inch Touraine Shade (Dresden Decoration), $20.00

Plate 439. Touraine shade. *Dresden* decoration #873. Base #D3000/873 (matching glass base). 1915.

OLD BRASS, EGYPTIAN BRASS, FLEMISH, ANTIQUE AND BRONZE FINISH.

THE PAIRPOINT CORPORATION
NEW BEDFORD, MASS.
43-47 West 23rd St., New York City
Hammond Bldg., 278 Post St.,
San Francisco, Cal.
228 Coristine Building, St. Nicholas St.,
NEG. 348. Montreal, Can.

Base D 3074—12 inch, 2 Light..............$12.00
16 inch Touraine Shade, No. 336............ 14.00
Decoration: Vogue. $26.00

Base D 3074—12 inch, 3 Light..............$13.35
16 inch Touraine Shade, No. 336............ 14.00
Decoration: Vogue. $27.35

Height to Top of Shade, 21½ inches.

Plate 440. Touraine shade. Vogue decoration #336. Base #D3074. 1926.

THE PAIRPOINT CORPORATION,
NEW BEDFORD, MASS.
38 Murray Street, New York City.
Coristine Building, St. Nicholas St.,
Montreal, Canada.
717 Market St., San Francisco, Cal.
NEG. 663

ELECTRIC CEILING BOWL.

Height from Ceiling to Bottom of Globe, 28½ inches.
With Three Light Fixture and Chain, Finished in Old Brass.
Wired Complete with Sockets.

No. 724. 12 inch Touraine, $19.10

Plate 441. Touraine shade. Ceiling bowl. *Jasper with Wedgwood urn* decoration #724. 1910-1914.

No. C 3073. ELECTROLIER. With 8 Feet Silk Cord, Height of Body, 10 inches.
Special One Light Fixture, Less Shade, Plain Old Brass, Antique or Gun Metal, $10.50

THE PAIRPOINT CORPORATION,
NEW BEDFORD, MASS.
38 Murray Street, New York City.
Coristine Building, St. Nicholas St.,
Montreal, Canada.
717 Market St., San Francisco, Cal.
NEG. 580

No. 726. 12 inch Special Touraine Shade, $6.85

TRADE MARK

Plate 442. Touraine shade. Special. *Country scene* decoration #726. Base #C3073. 1910-1914.

No. B 3026.   ELECTROLIER, with 8 Feet Silk Cord, Height of Body, 11 inches.

THE PAIRPOINT CORPORATION,
NEW BEDFORD, MASS.
38 Murray Street, New York City.
485 St. Catherine St., Montreal, Canada.
717 Market St., San Francisco, Cal.
Neg. 639 A

One Light, Less Shade, Copper, Metal Trimmings, $13.00
Two   "   "   "   "   "   "   17.00
No. 1220. 12 inch Touraine Shade, $7.00

Plate 443. Touraine shade. *Rose hip* decoration #1220. Base #B3026. 1907-1910.

No. B 3027. ELECTROLIER, with 8 Feet Silk Cord, Height of Body, 10 inches.

THE PAIRPOINT CORPORATION,
NEW BEDFORD, MASS.
38 Murray Street, New York City.
485 St. Catherine St., Montreal, Canada.
717 Market St., San Francisco, Cal.
Neg. 665 A

One Light, Less Shade, Copper, Gray Finish, $13.00
Two   "   "   "   "   "   17.00

No. 981. 12 inch Touraine Shade, $5.50

Plate 444. Touraine shade. *Daffodil.* #981. Base #B3027. 1907-1910.

No. B 3035. ELECTROLIER, with 8 Feet Silk Cord, Height of Body, 10 inches.

THE PAIRPOINT CORPORATION,
NEW BEDFORD, MASS.
38 Murray Street, New York City.
485 St. Catherine St., Montreal, Canada.
717 Market St., San Francisco, Cal.
Neg. 669 A

One Light, Less Shade, Engraved, Old Brass, $12.50
Two "   "   "   "   "   16.50

No. 1553. 12 inch Touraine Shade, $9.50

Plate 445. Touraine shade. *Royal Flemish style griffin with cherub* decoration #1553. Base #B3035. 1907-1910.

No. C 3023. ELECTROLIER, with 8 Feet Silk Cord, Height of Body, 9 inches.
Special Two Light Fixture

THE PAIRPOINT CORPORATION,
NEW BEDFORD, MASS.
38 Murray Street, New York City.
Coristine Building, St. Nicholas St.,
Montreal, Canada.
717 Market St., San Francisco, Cal.
Neg. 445

Plain, ~~One Light~~ Less Shade, Old Brass, Antique or Gun Metal, $10.50
Engraved, "   "   "   "   "   "   "   "   "   12.00
"   "   "   "   Plain Silver, $11.50
"   "   "   "   Engraved,   13.00
Fancy Coloring, $1.50 Extra.

No. 654. 12 inch Touraine Shade, $8.20

Plate 446. Touraine shade. *Hollyhocks and scroll border* decoration #654 (open top). Base #C3023. 1910-1914.

No. C 3058 ELECTROLIER, with 8 Feet Silk Cord, Height of Body, 8 inches.
Special Two Light Fixture, Less Shade, Old Brass Green, Antique or Gun Metal, $6.85

THE PAIRPOINT CORPORATION,
NEW BEDFORD, MASS.
38 Murray Street, New York City.
Coristine Building, St. Nicholas St.,
Montreal, Canada.
717 Market St., San Francisco, Cal.
NEG. 446

No. 653   12 inch Touraine Shade, $5.50

Plate 447. Touraine shade. *Dandelion* decoration #653 (open top). Base #C3058. 1910-1914.

No. C 3060. ELECTROLIER, with 8 Feet Silk Cord. Height of Body, 10 inches.
Plain. One Light. Less Shade, Old Brass Green, Antique or Gun Metal, $7.75

THE PAIRPOINT CORPORATION,
NEW BEDFORD, MASS.
38 Murray Street, New York City.
Coristine Building, St. Nicholas St.,
Montreal, Canada.
717 Market St., San Francisco, Cal.
Neg. 348

No. 505. 12 inch Louraine Shade. $5.00

TRADE MARK

Plate 448. Touraine shade. *Winter village scene* decoration #505. Base #C3060. 1910-1914.

No. C 3065.   ELECTROLIER.   With 8 Feet Silk Cord, Height of Body, 10 inches.
Special Two Light Fixture, Less Shade, Old Brass Green, Antique or Gun Metal, $8.65

THE PAIRPOINT CORPORATION,
NEW BEDFORD, MASS.
38 Murray Street, New York City.
Coristine Building, St. Nicholas St.,
Montreal, Canada.
717 Market St., San Francisco, Cal.
Neg. 582

No. 728.   12 inch Touraine Shade, $13.20

TRADE MARK

Plate 449. Touraine shade. *Cupid with jasper background* decoration #728 (open top). Base #C3065. 1910-1914.

No. C 3065. ELECTROLIER. With 8 Feet Silk Cord, Height of Body, 10 inches.
Special Two Light Fixture, Less Shade, Old Brass Green, Antique or Gun Metal, $8.65

THE PAIRPOINT CORPORATION,
NEW BEDFORD, MASS.
38 Murray Street, New York City.
Coristine Building, St. Nicholas St.,
Montreal, Canada.
717 Market St., San Francisco, Cal.
Neg. 591

No. 725. 12 inch Touraine Shade, $9.10

TRADE MARK

Plate 450. Touraine shade. *Lyre and laurel* decoration #725 (open top). Base #C3065. 1910-1914.

No. B3025.   ELECTROLIER, with 8 Feet Silk Cord, Height of Body, 8½ inches.

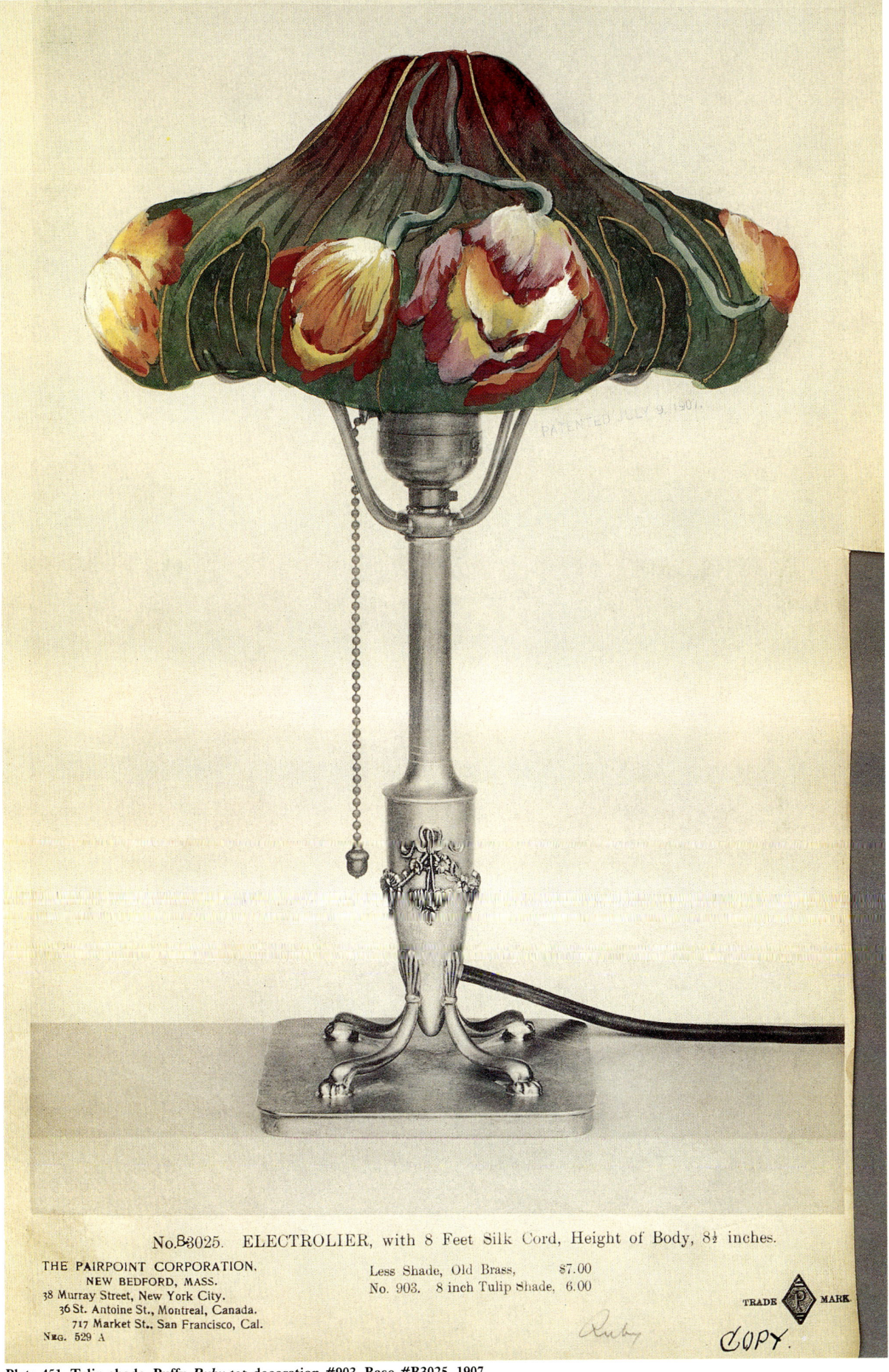

THE PAIRPOINT CORPORATION,
NEW BEDFORD, MASS.
38 Murray Street, New York City.
36 St. Antoine St., Montreal, Canada.
717 Market St., San Francisco, Cal.

Less Shade, Old Brass, $7.00
No. 903. 8 inch Tulip Shade. 6.00

Plate 451. Tulip shade. Puffy. *Ruby top* decoration #903. Base #B3025. 1907.

No. B 3023. ELECTROLIER, with 8 Feet Silk Cord, Height of Body, 8 inches.

THE PAIRPOINT CORPORATION.
NEW BEDFORD, MASS.
38 Murray Street, New York City.
485 St. Catherine St., Montreal, Canada.
717 Market St., San Francisco, Cal.
NEG 727 A

Less Shade, Old Brass, Plain, $6.00
"   "   Engraved, 7.50
No. 902 8 inch Tulip Shade, $6.00

Plate 452. Tulip shade. Puffy. *Tulip* decoration #902. Base #B3023. 1907-1910.

Plate 453. Tulip shade. Puffy. *Tulip* decoration #902; Portsmouth shades. *Stylized leaves and tulips* decoration #1368; *Orchids* decoration #1384; *Flemish Clematis* decoration #1387. No date.

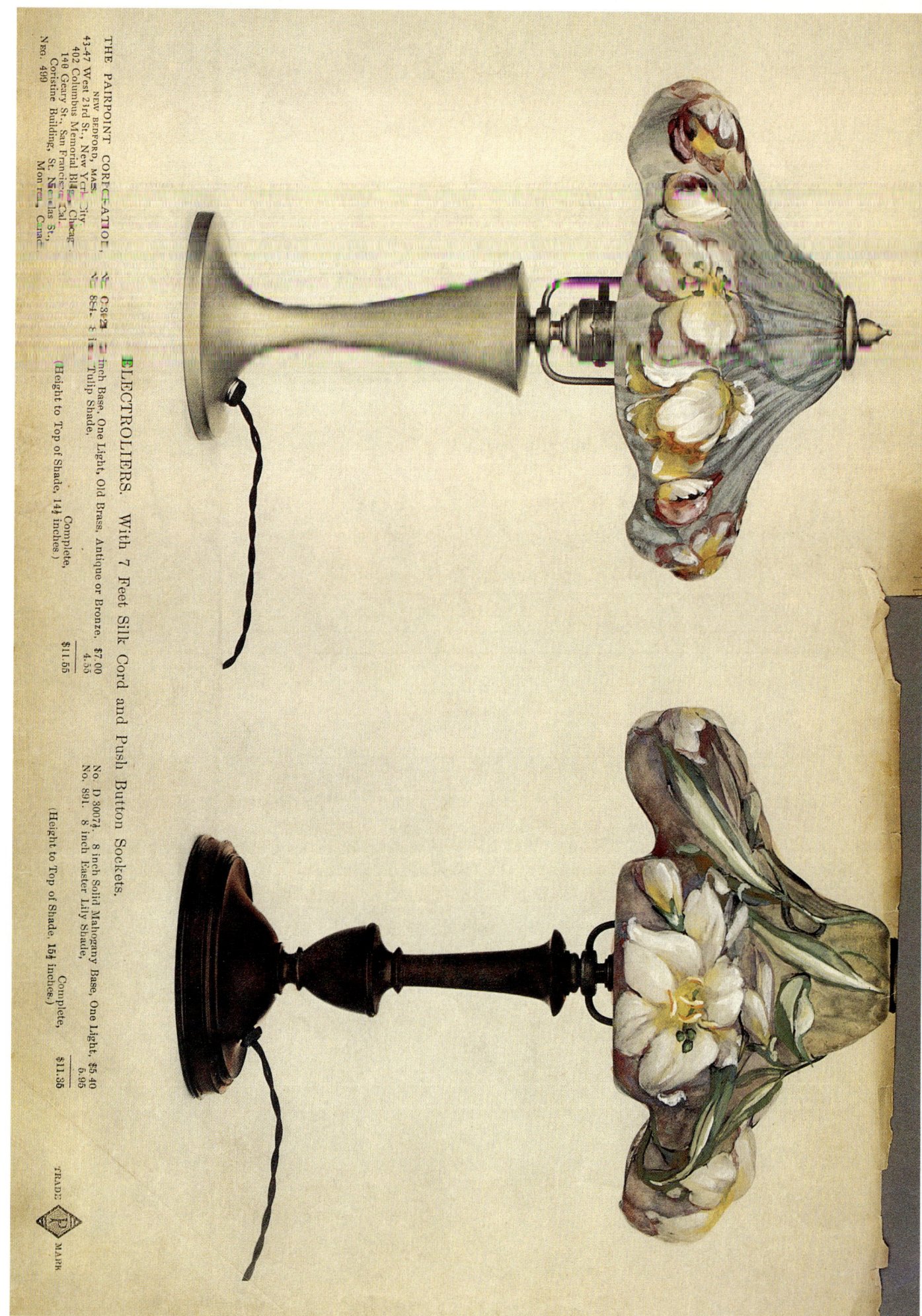

Plate 454. Tulip shade. Puffy. *Tulip* decoration #884 (open top). Base #C3024; Easter Lily shade. *Easter Lily* decoration #891 (open top). Base #D3007 1/2. 1915.

No. C 3042.   ELECTROLIER, with 8 Feet Silk Cord.   Height of Body, 11¼ inches.

Plain,	One Light, Less Shade, Old Brass, Antique or Gun Metal,		$14.55	Two Lights,	$17.30
	"	"	Green or Gun Metal,	18.20	"	20.95
Engraved,	"	"	"	"	"	19.15
	"	"	French Grey,	$16.40	"	
	"	"	Engraved, French Grey,	20.00	"	22.75

THE PAIRPOINT CORPORATION,
NEW BEDFORD, MASS.
38 Murray Street, New York City.
Coristine Building, St. Nicholas St.,
Montreal, Canada.
717 Market St., San Francisco, Cal.

Fancy Coloring, $1.40 Extra.

No. 1235. 14 inch Tuscanna Shade, $18.20

TRADE MARK

NEG. 346

Plate 455. Tuscanna shade. *Roses* decoration #1235. Base #C3042. 1910-1914.

No. C 3045.   ELECTROLIER, with 8 Feet Silk Cord.   Height of Body, 13½ inches.

Plain,	One Light, Less Shade, Old Brass. Antique or Gun Metal,		$15.50	Two Lights,	$18.25
Engraved,	" " "	Green and Red or Gun Metal,	17.30	"	20.05
" "	" " "	French Grey,	$17.30	"	20.05
" "	" " "	Engraved, French Grey,	19.10	"	21.85

Fancy Coloring, $ .95 Extra.

No. 1272. 14 inch Tuscanna Shade, $11.85

THE PAIRPOINT CORPORATION.
NEW BEDFORD, MASS.
38 Murray Street, New York City.
Coristine Building, St. Nicholas St.,
Montreal, Canada.
717 Market St., San Francisco, Cal.

Neg. 384

TRADE MARK

Plate 456. Tuscanna shade. *Poppy tapestry* decoration #1272. Base #C3045. 1910-1914.

No. C 3047. ELECTROLIER, with 8 Feet Silk Cord. Height of Body, 13 inches.

	Plain,	One Light, Less Shade, Old Brass, Antique or Gun Metal,	$15.50	Two Lights,	$18.25
	Engraved,	" " " Green or Gun Metal,	18.20	"	20.95
	" "	" " French Grey,	$17.30	"	20.05
	" "	Engraved, French Grey,	20.00	"	22.75

Fancy Coloring, $1.40 Extra.

THE PAIRPOINT CORPORATION,
NEW BEDFORD, MASS.
38 Murray Street, New York City,
Coristine Building, St. Nicholas St.,
Montreal, Canada.
717 Market St., San Francisco, Cal.
NEG. 367

No. 1234. 14 inch Tuscanna Shade, $13.65

TRADE MARK

Plate 457. Tuscanna shade. *Floral panel border* decoration #1234. Base #C3047. 1910-1914.

No. C 3074/723. ELECTRIC URN. With 7 Feet Silk Cord, Wired Complete, $30.00

THE PAIRPOINT CORPORATION,
NEW BEDFORD, MASS.
38 Murray Street, New York City.
Coristine Building, St. Nicholas St.,
Montreal, Canada.
717 Market St., San Francisco, Cal.
NEG. 653

Diameter, 12 inches. Height, 19 inches
Fitted with Three Light Cluster.
Finished in Old Brass

TRADE

Plate 458. Electric Urn. *Classical Jasper* decoration #723. Base #C3074/723 (matching glass base). 1910-1914.

No. C 3074/781.   ELECTRIC URN.   With 7 Feet Silk Cord, Complete, $30.00

THE PAIRPOINT CORPORATION,
NEW BEDFORD, MASS.
38 Murray Street, New York City.
Coristine Building, St. Nicholas St.,
Montreal, Canada.
717 Market St., San Francisco, Cal.
NEG. 712

Diameter, 12 inches.   Height 19 inches.
Fitted with Three Light Cluster and Finished in Old Brass.

TRADE

Plate 459. Electric Urn. *Jasper Urn* decoration #781. Base #C3074/781 (matching glass base). 1910-1914.

No. C 3079/774. ELECTRIC URN. With 7 Feet Silk Cord, Wired Complete, $36.40

AIRPOINT CORPORATION,
NEW BEDFORD, MASS.
Street, New York City.
Building, St. Nicholas St.,
      Montreal, Canada.
rket St., San Francisco, Cal.

Diameter, 12 inches.   Height, 17 inches.
Fitted with Three Light Cluster and Finished in Old Brass.

Plate 460. Electric Urn. *Floral garland* decoration #774. Base #C3079/774 (matching glass base). No date.

No. D 3005/880. ELECTRIC URN.
With Mahogany Pedestal, Wired with 8 Feet Silk Cord, Complete, $36.40

THE PAIRPOINT CORPORATION,
NEW BEDFORD, MASS.
43-47 West 23rd St., New York City.
402 Columbus Memorial Bldg., Chicago.
140 Geary St., San Francisco, Cal.
Coristine Building, St. Nicholas St.,
NEG. 996   Montreal, Canada.

Height to Top of Urn, 29½ inches.
Fitted with Three Light Cluster.

TRADE P MARK

Plate 461. Electric Urn. *Cameo* decoration #880. Base #D3005/880 (mahogany pedestal). No date.

No. D 3005/880. ELECTRIC URN.
With Mahogany Pedestal, Wired with 8 Feet Silk Cord, Complete, $36.40

THE PAIRPOINT CORPORATION,
NEW BEDFORD, MASS.
43-47 West 23rd St., New York City.
402 Columbus Memorial Bldg., Chicago.
140 Geary St., San Francisco, Cal.
Coristine Building, St. Nicholas St.,
NEG. 996   Montreal, Canada.

Height to Top of Urn, 29½ inches.
Fitted with Three Light Cluster.

TRADE MARK

Plate 462. Electric Urn. *Cameo* decoration #880. Base #D3005/880 (mahogany pedestal). 1915.

No. D 3005/881.   ELECTRIC URN.
With Mahogany Pedestal, Wired with 8 Feet Silk Cord, Complete, $36.40

THE PAIRPOINT CORPORATION,
NEW BEDFORD, MASS.
43-47 West 23rd St., New York City.
402 Columbus Memorial Bldg., Chicago.
140 Geary St., San Francisco, Cal.
Coristine Building, St. Nicholas St.,
Neg. 997   Montreal, Canada.

Height to Top of Urn, 29½ inches.
Fitted with Three Light Cluster.

TRADE

Plate 463. Electric Urn. *Rosette and swag* decoration #881. Base #D3005/881 (mahogany pedestal). 1915.

THE PAIRPOINT CORPORATION,
NEW BEDFORD, MASS.
38 Murray Street, New York City.
Coristine Building, St. Nicholas St.,
Montreal, Canada.
717 Market St., San Francisco, Cal.
NEG. 654

ELECTRIC CEILING BOWL.

Height from Ceiling to Bottom of Globe, 29½ inches.
With Four Light Fixture and Chain, Finished in Old Brass.
Wired Complete with Sockets.

No. 729.   12 inch Venice, $27.30

Plate 464. Venice shade. Ceiling fixture. *Frolicking cherubs tapestry* **decoration #729. 1910-1914.**

No. B 3019. ELECTROLIER, with 8 Feet Silk Cord, Height of Body, 14 inches.

THE PAIRPOINT CORPORATION,
NEW BEDFORD, MASS.
38 Murray Street, New York City.
485 St. Catherine St., Montreal, Canada.
727 Market St., San Francisco, Cal.

Less Shade, Old Brass, Antique Green, Gun Metal or Copper, $13.50
Two Lights, $4.00 extra.
No. 965. 12 inch Venice Shade, $12.00

Plate 465. Venice shade. *Rose tapestry* decoration #965. Base #B3019. 1907-1910.

Plate 466. Venice shade. *Whirling leaves* decoration #966. Base #B3030. No date.

No. B 3040.   ELECTROLIER, with 8 Feet Silk Cord, Height of Body, 12 inches.

THE PAIRPOINT CORPORATION.
NEW BEDFORD, MASS.
38 Murray Street, New York City.
485 St. Catherine St., Montreal, Canada.
717 Market St., San Francisco, Cal.
NEG 806 A

Less Shade, Old Brass, Antique Green, Gun Metal or Copper, $15.00

Two Lights, $4.00 extra.

No. 964.   12 inch Venice Shade, $12.00

Plate 467. Venice shade. *Tulip* decoration #964. Base #B3040. 1907-1910.

No. B 3065.   ELECTROLIER, with 8 Feet Silk Cord.   Height of Body, 16 inches.

One Light, Less Shade, Plain Old Brass Green, Gun Metal or Antique, $18.00   Two Light, $22.00
" "   Engraved, Old Brass Green and Red, or Gun Metal,   19.00   "   23.00

THE PAIRPOINT CORPORATION,
NEW BEDFORD, MASS.
38 Murray Street, New York City.
Coristine Building, St. Nicholas St.,
Montreal, Canada.
717 Market St., San Francisco, Cal.

No. 908 A. 12 inch Venice Shade, $9.00

NEG. 961 A

TRADE MARK

Plate 468. Venice shade. *Pansies* decoration #908A. Base #B3065. 1910-1914.

No. C 3069/709. ELECTROLIER. With 8 Feet Silk Cord, Height of Body, 16½ inches. Complete, $22.7[5]
Lamp Base, Less Shade, with Special Two Light Fixture, Old Brass Trimmings, $13.65

THE PAIRPOINT CORPORATION,
NEW BEDFORD, MASS.
38 Murray Street, New York City.
Coristine Building, St. Nicholas St.,
Montreal, Canada.
717 Market St., San Francisco, Cal.

No. 709. 14 inch Vienna Shade, $9.10

NEG. 552

TRADE MARK

Plate 469. Vienna shade. *Olympic torch* decoration #709. Base #C3069/709 (matching glass base). 1910-1914.

No. C 3069/708.   ELECTROLIER.   With 8 Feet Silk Cord, Height of Body, 16½ inches.   Complete, $22.3

Lamp Base, Less Shade, with Special Two Light Fixture, Old Brass Trimmings, $13.20

THE PAIRPOINT CORPORATION,
NEW BEDFORD, MASS.
38 Murray Street, New York City.
Coristine Building, St. Nicholas St.,
Montreal, Canada.
717 Market St., San Francisco, Cal.

No. 708. 14 inch Vienna Shade, $9.10

NEG. 553

TRADE MARK

Plate 470. Vienna shade. *Green leather with rosebud* decoration #708. Base #C3069/708 (matching glass base). 1910-1914.

No. C 3069/707. ELECTROLIER. With 8 Feet Silk Cord, Height of Body, 16½ inches. Complete, $23

Lamp Base, Less Shade, with Special Two Light Fixture, Old Brass Trimmings, $13.65

THE PAIRPOINT CORPORATION,
NEW BEDFORD, MASS.
38 Murray Street, New York City.
Coristine Building, St. Nicholas St.,
Montreal, Canada.
717 Market St., San Francisco, Cal.

No. 707. 14 inch Vienna Shade, $10.00

NRG. 589

TRADE P MARK

Plate 471. Vienna shade. *Red leather* decoration #707. Base #C3069/707 (matching glass base). No date.

THE PAIRPOINT CORPORATION,
NEW BEDFORD, MASS.
38 Murray Street, New York City.
Coristine Building, St. Nicholas St.,
Montreal, Canada.
717 Market St., San Francisco, Cal.
NEG. 655

ELECTRIC CEILING BOWL.
Height from Ceiling to Bottom of Globe, 28½ inches.
With Three Light Fixture and Chain, Finished in Old Brass.
Wired Complete, with Sockets.
No. 715. 14 inch Vienna, $21.85

TRADE

Plate 472. Vienna shade. Ceiling bowl. *Lyre and scroll* **decoration #715. 1910-1914.**

THE PAIRPOINT CORPORATION,
NEW BEDFORD, MASS.
38 Murray Street, New York City.
Coristine Building, St. Nicholas St.,
Montreal, Canada.
717 Market St., San Francisco, Cal.

NEG. 661

ELECTRIC CEILING BOWL.

Height from Ceiling to Bottom of Globe, 28½ inches.
With Three Light Fixture and Chain, Finished in Old Brass.
Wired Complete with Sockets.

No. 710. 14 inch Vienna, $21.85

Plate 473. Vienna shade. Ceiling bowl. *Floral bouquet with lattice* decoration #710. 1910-1914.

Plate 474 and 475. Vienna shade. Ceiling bowl. *Jasper* decoration #712. 1910-1914.

THE PAIRPOINT CORPORATION,
NEW BEDFORD, MASS.
38 Murray Street, New York City.
Coristine Building, St. Nicholas St.,
Montreal, Canada.
717 Market St., San Francisco, Cal.
NEG. 667

ELECTRIC CEILING BOWL.

Height from Ceiling to Bottom of Globe, 28½ inches.
With Three Light Fixture and Chain. Finished in Old Brass.
Wired Complete with Sockets.

No. 713. 14 inch Vienna.

Plate 476. Vienna shade. Ceiling bowl. *Green leather with rosebud* decoration #713. 1910-1914.

THE PAIRPOINT CORPORATION,
NEW BEDFORD, MASS.
38 Murray Street, New York City.
Coristine Building, St. Nicholas St.,
Montreal, Canada.
717 Market St., San Francisco, Cal.
NEG. 674

ELECTRIC CEILING BOWLS.

Height from Ceiling to Bottom of Globe, 28½ inches.
With Three Light Fixture and Chain, Finished in Old Brass,
Wired Complete, with Sockets.
No. 711. 14 inch Vienna, $21.85

Plate 477. Vienna shade. Ceiling bowl. *Jasper classical female figure in medallion* **decoration #711. 1910-1914.**

THE PAIRPOINT CORPORATION,
NEW BEDFORD, MASS.
38 Murray Street, New York City.
Coristine Building, St. Nicholas St.,
Montreal, Canada.
717 Market St., San Francisco, Cal.
NEG. 675

ELECTRIC CEILING BOWLS.
Height from Ceiling to Bottom of Globe, 28½ inches.
With Three Light Fixture and Chain, Finished in Old Brass,
Wired Complete, with Sockets.
No. 714. 14 inch Vienna, $24.55

TRADE

Plate 478. Vienna shade. Ceiling bowl. *Jasper cameo* decoration #714. 1910-1914.

Plate 479. Vienna shade (centre piece). *Dutch village* decoration #705. Base #C3072 (with planter inset). 1910-1914.

No. C 3072.

THE PAIRPOINT CORPORATION,
NEW BEDFORD, MASS.
38 Murray Street, New York City.
Corbine Building, St. Nicholas St., Montreal, Canada.
717 Market St., San Francisco, Cal.
Neg. 561

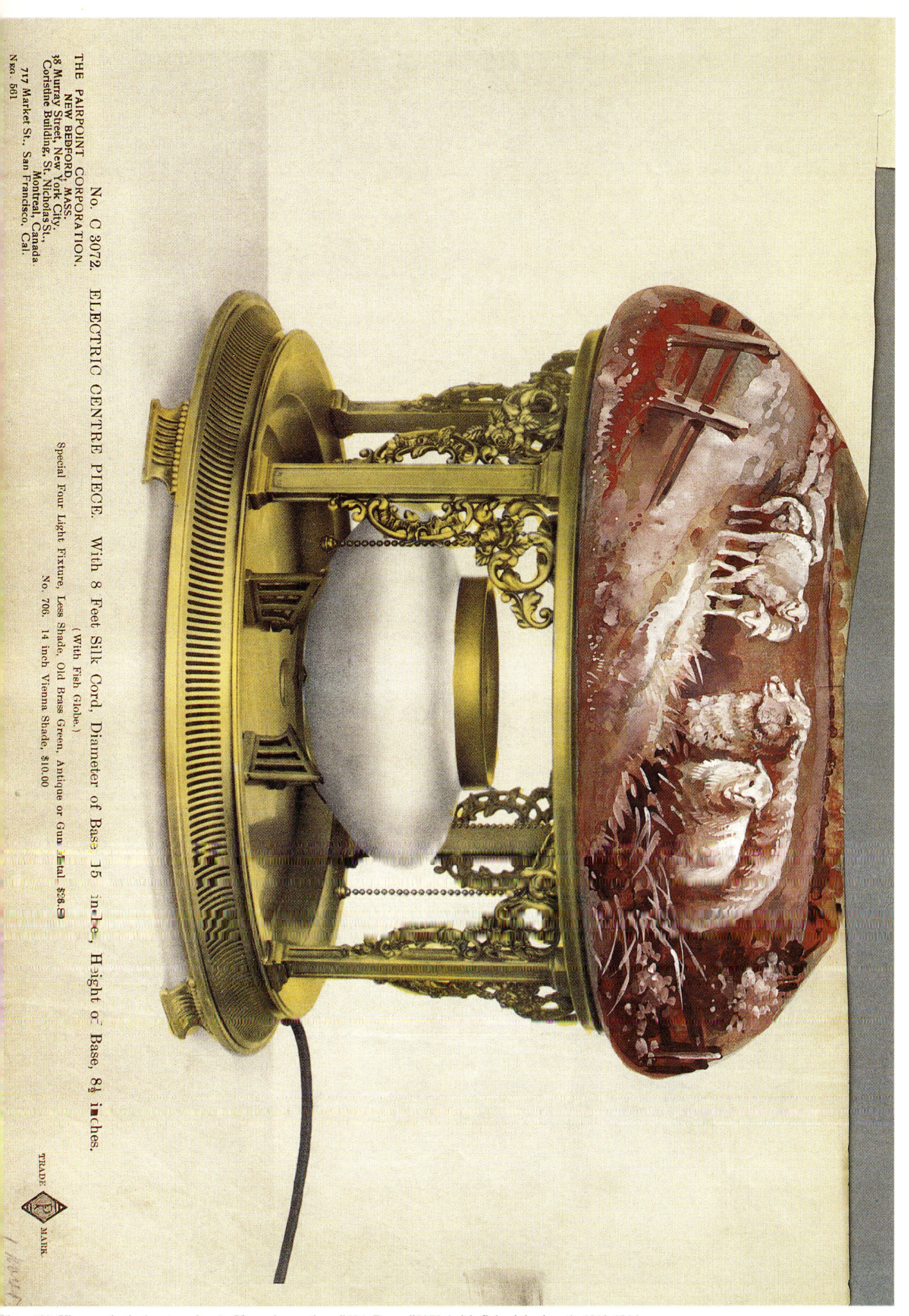

ELECTRIC CENTRE PIECE. With 8 Feet Silk Cord, Diameter of Base 15 inches, Height of Base, 8½ inches.
(With Fish Globe.)
Special Four Light Fixture, Less Shade, Old Brass Green, Antique or Gun Metal, $28.9
No. 706. 14 inch Vienna Shade, $10.00

TRADE P MARK

Plate 480. Vienna shade (centre piece). *Sheep* decoration #706. Base #3072 (with fish globe inset). 1910-1914.

No. B 3095.   ELECTROLIER.   With 8 Feet Silk Cord, Height of Body, 11 inches.
One Light, Less Shade, Old Brass Green, Antique Green or Gun Metal. With Tripod, $9.50. With 10 inch Ring, $8.00

THE PAIRPOINT CORPORATION,
NEW BEDFORD, MASS.
38 Murray Street, New York City.
Coristine Building, St. Nicholas St.,
Montreal, Canada.
717 Market St., San Francisco, Cal.
NEG 81

Two Light, $4.00 extra.

No. 1545.   10 inch Vienna Shade, $8.00

TRADE

Plate 481. Vienna shade. *Bearded iris* decoration #1545. Base #B3095. 1910-1914.

Plate 482. Vienna shade. *Cyclamen leaves* decoration #966. Base #3041 (with screw-in socket). No date.

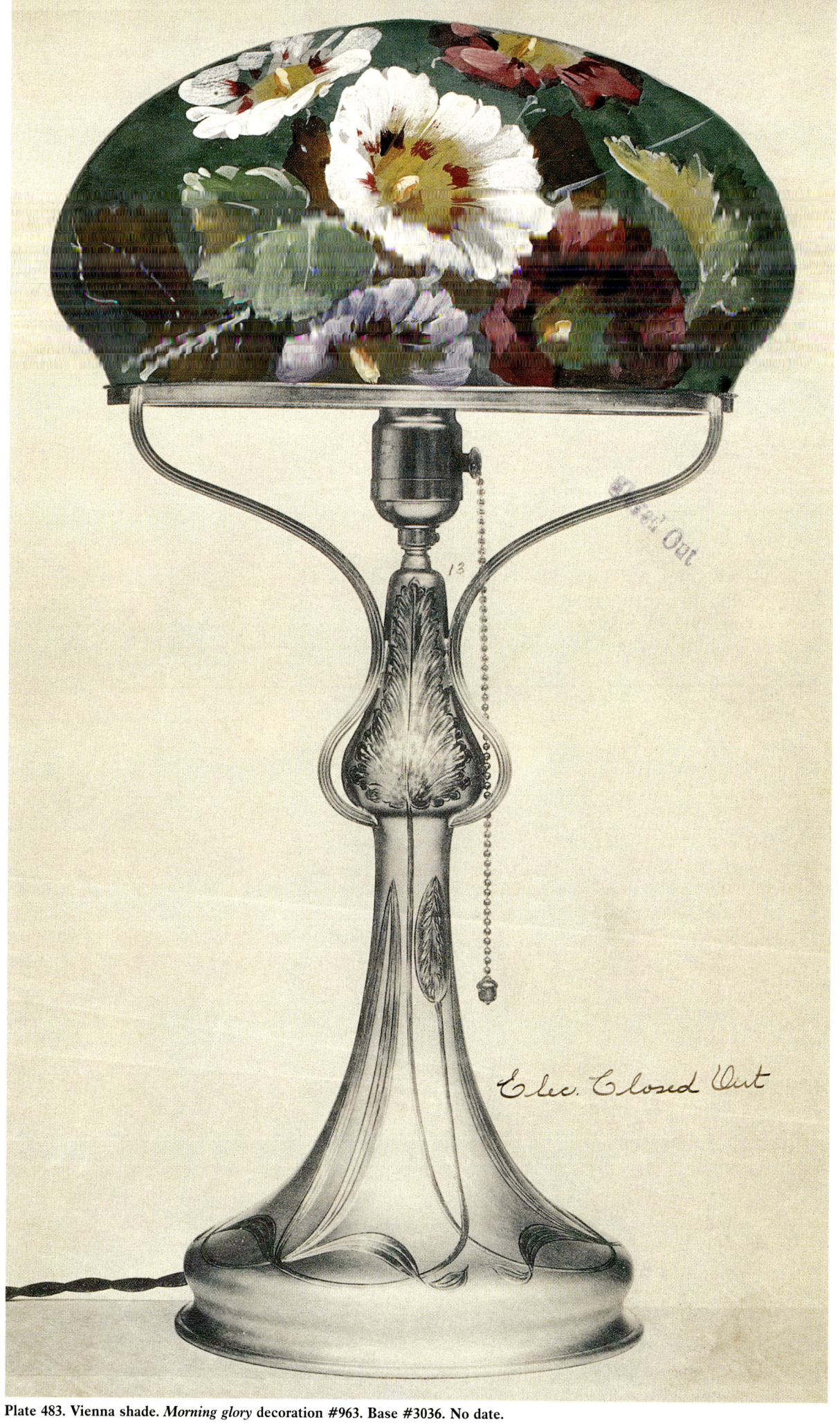

Plate 483. Vienna shade. *Morning glory* decoration #963. Base #3036. No date.

Plate 484. Vienna shade. *Lilac* decoration #1232. Base #3040. No date.

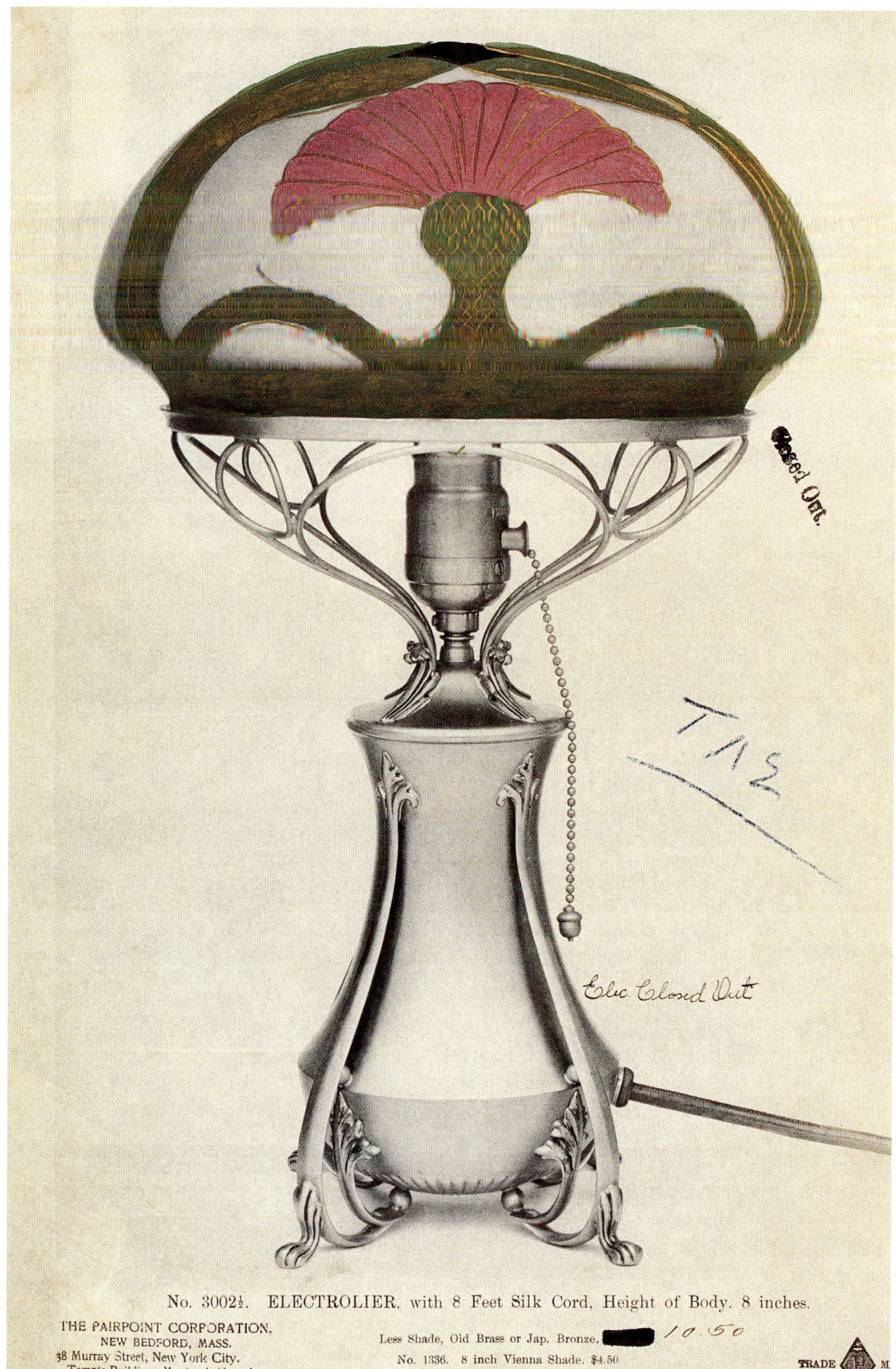

No. 3002½. ELECTROLIER, with 8 Feet Silk Cord, Height of Body, 8 inches.

THE PAIRPOINT CORPORATION.
NEW BEDFORD, MASS.
38 Murray Street, New York City.
Temple Building, Montreal, Canada.
220 Sutter Street, San Francisco, Cal.
NEG. 270 A

Less Shade, Old Brass or Jap. Bronze.
No. 1336. 8 inch Vienna Shade. $4.50

QUADRUPLE PLATE.

Plate 485. Vienna shade. *Nouveau thistle* decoration #1336. Base #3002 1/2. 1900-1903.

Plate 486. Vienna shade. *Poppy* decoration #931. Base #3003 1/2. 1900-1903.

No. 3009½. ELECTROLIER, with 8 Feet Silk Cord, Height of Body, 8 inches.

THE PAIRPOINT CORPORATION,
NEW BEDFORD, MASS.
38 Murray Street, New York City.
Temple Building, Montreal, Canada.
220 Sutter Street, San Francisco, Cal.
NEG. 272 A

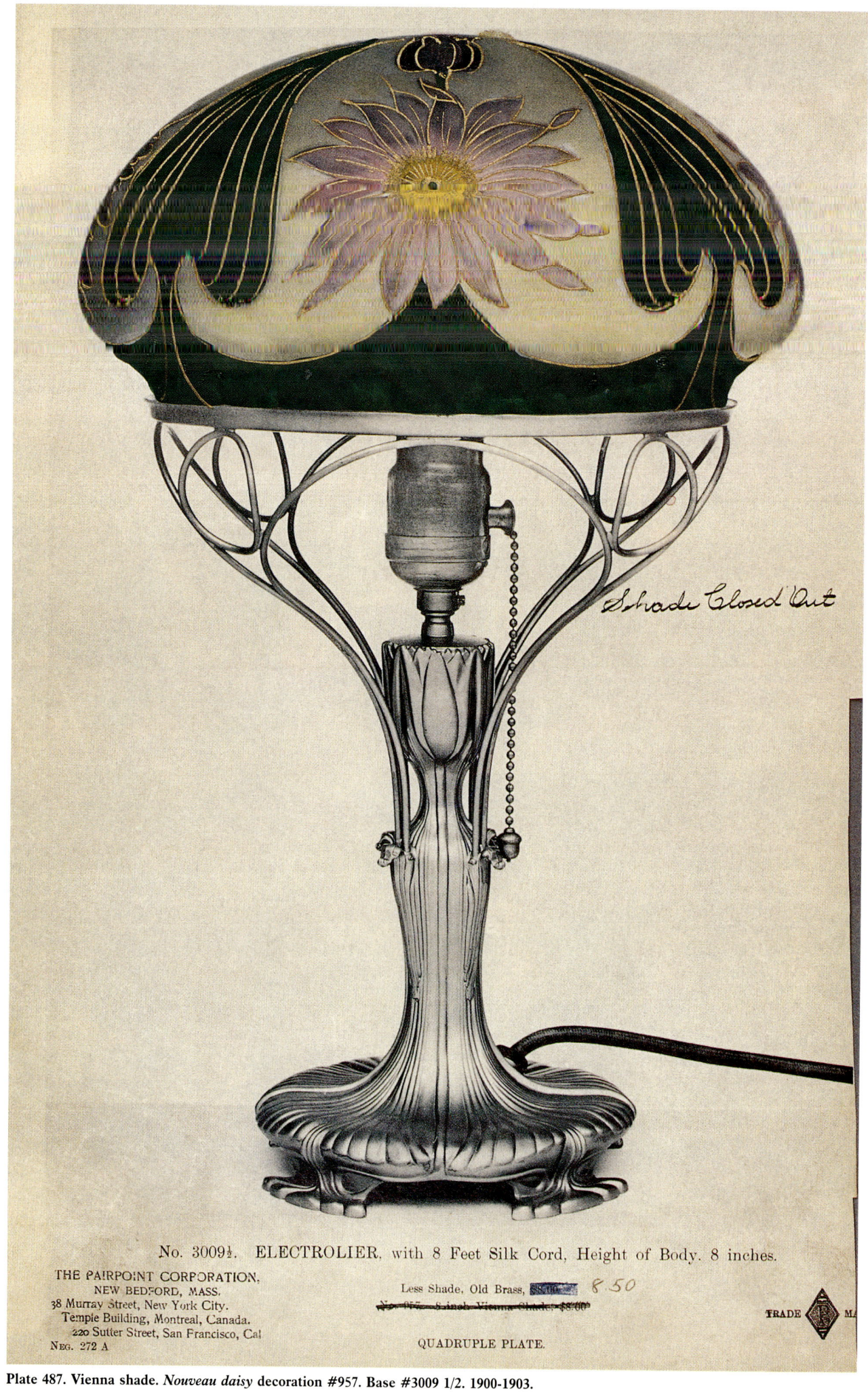

Less Shade, Old Brass, ~~$8.00~~ 8.50

QUADRUPLE PLATE.

Plate 487. Vienna shade. *Nouveau daisy* decoration #957. Base #3009 1/2. 1900-1903.

No. 3030½ ELECTROLIER, with 8 Feet of Silk Cord, Height of Body, 9 inches.

THE PAIRPOINT CORPORATION,
NEW BEDFORD, MASS.
38 Murray Street, New York City.
Temple Building, Montreal, Canada.
220 Sutter Street, San Francisco, Cal.
NEG. 275 A

Less Shade, Plain, Old Brass or Jap. Bronze $7.50
"   "   Engraved,   "   "   "   8.50
No. 1334. 8 inch Vienna Shade,   6.00

QUADRUPLE PLATE.

TRADE MARK

Plate 488. Vienna shade. *Ivy leaves* decoration #1334. Base #3030 1/2. 1900-1903.

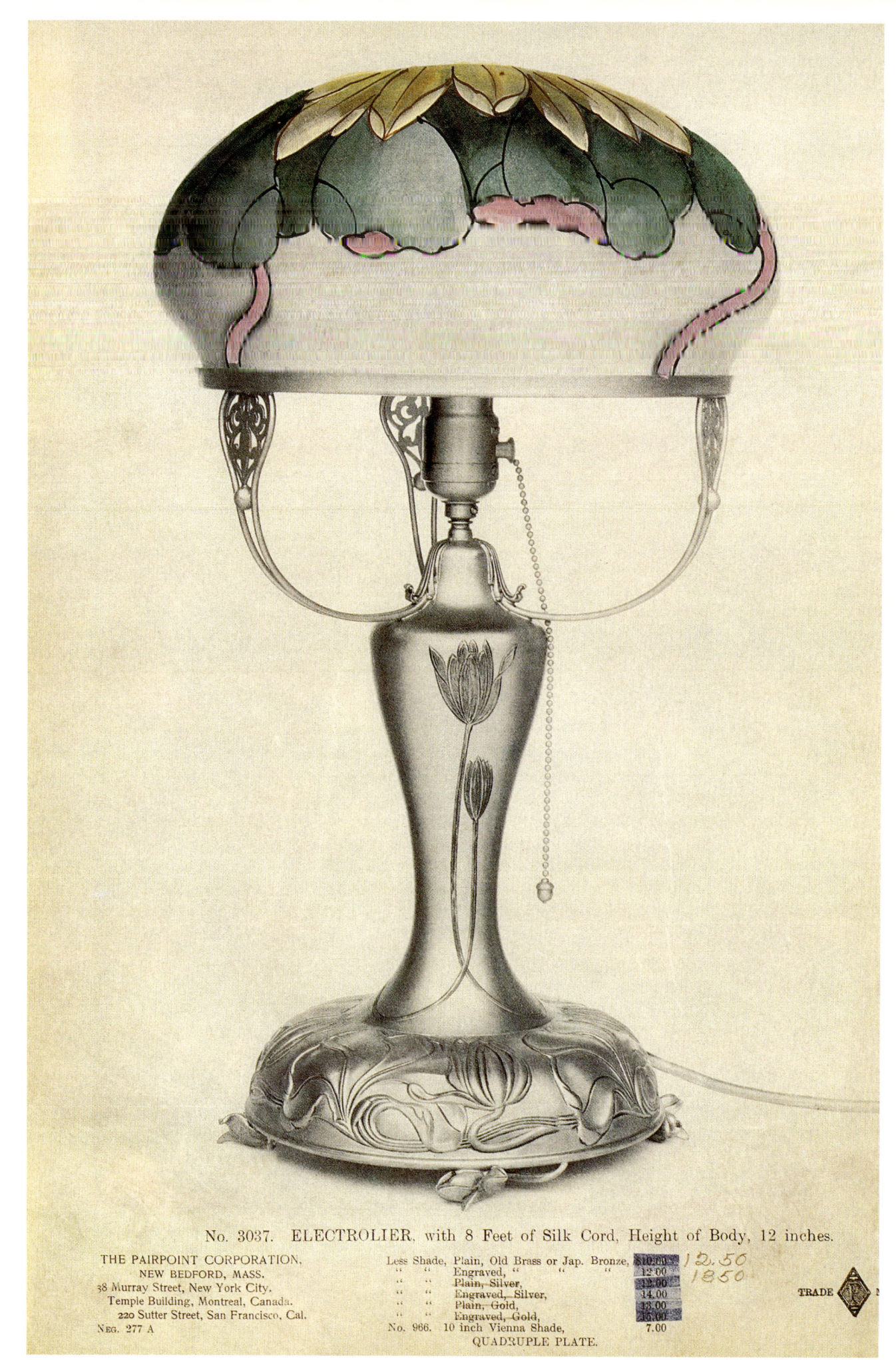

No. 3037. ELECTROLIER, with 8 Feet of Silk Cord, Height of Body, 12 inches.

THE PAIRPOINT CORPORATION,
NEW BEDFORD, MASS.
38 Murray Street, New York City.
Temple Building, Montreal, Canada.
220 Sutter Street, San Francisco, Cal.
NEG. 277 A

Less Shade, Plain, Old Brass or Jap. Bronze, 10.00
" " Engraved, " " 12.00
" " Plain, Silver, 12.00
" " Engraved, Silver, 14.00
" " Plain, Gold, 13.00
" " Engraved, Gold, 16.00
No. 966. 10 inch Vienna Shade, 7.00
QUADRUPLE PLATE.

Plate 489. Vienna shade. *Nouveau Pond lily* decoration #966. Base #3037. 1900-1903.

No. 3038. ELECTROLIER, with 8 Feet of Silk Cord, Height of Body, 13 inches.

THE PAIRPOINT CORPORATION,
NEW BEDFORD, MASS.
38 Murray Street, New York City.
Temple Building, Montreal, Canada.
220 Sutter Street, San Francisco, Cal.
NEG. 278 A

Less Shade, Old Brass or Jap. Bronze, 12.50
    "   "   Silver, 12.50
    "   "   Gold, 18.50
No. 957. 10 inch Vienna Shade, 10.00

QUADRUPLE PLATE.

Plate 490. Vienna shade. *Nouveau daisy* decoration #957. Base #3038. 1900-1903.

Plate 491. Vienna shade. *Ivy leaves* decoration #1334. Base #3000 1/2. 1900-1903.

No. 3028½. ELECTROLIER, with 8 Feet of Silk Cord, Height of Body, 7½ inches.

THE PAIRPOINT CORPORATION,
NEW BEDFORD, MASS.
38 Murray Street, New York City.
Temple Building, Montreal, Canada.
220 Sutter Street, San Francisco, Cal.
NEG. 287 A

Less Shade, Plain, Old Brass or Jap. Bronze. 8.00 8 50
  "   "   Engraved,   "   "   "   9.00 9 00
No. 967. 8 inch Vienna Shade,   3.00

QUADRUPLE PLATE.

TRADE M

Plate 492. Vienna shade. *Raspberries and spider* decoration #967. #3028 1/2. 1900-1903

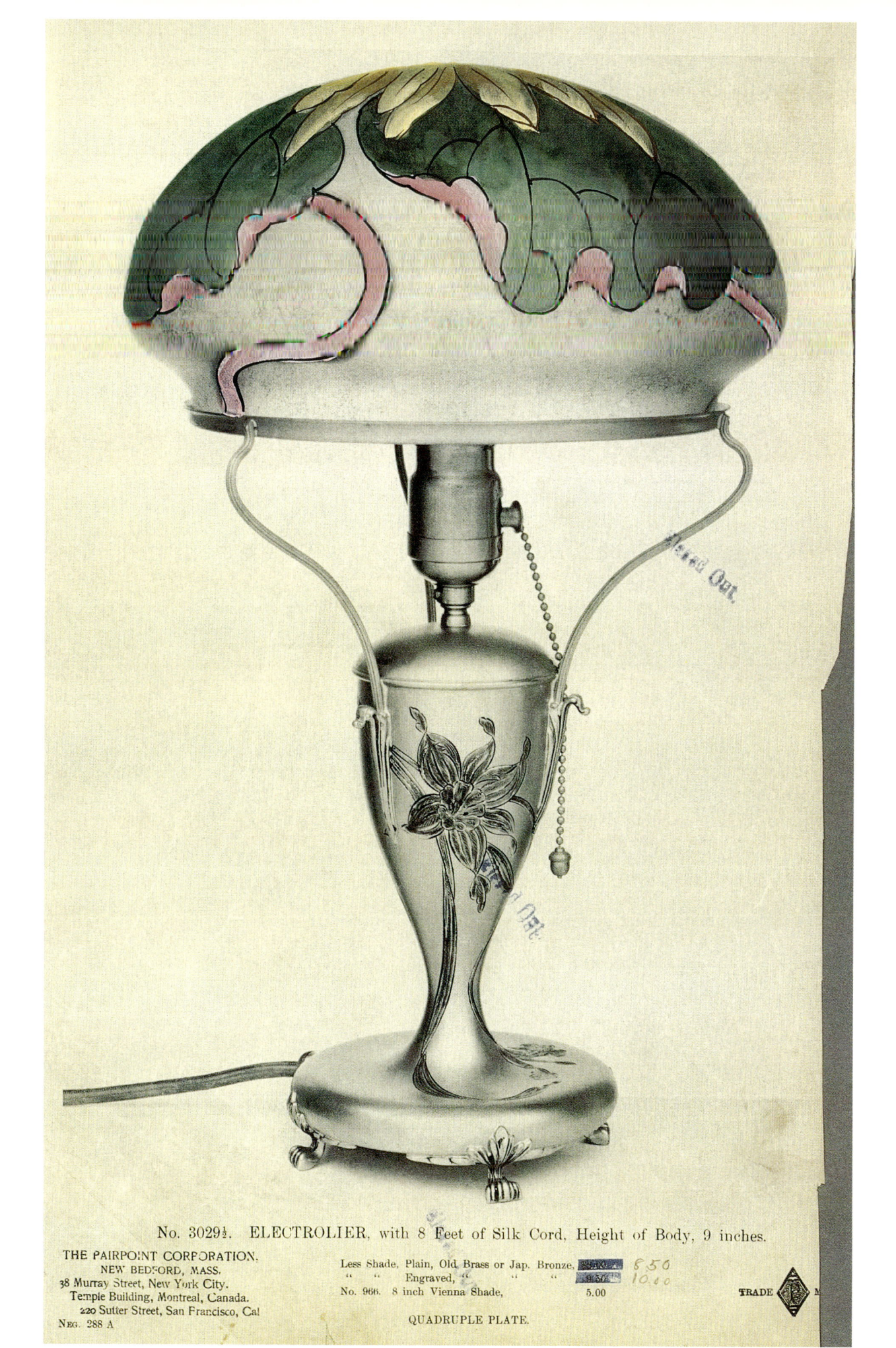

No. 3029½.   ELECTROLIER, with 8 Feet of Silk Cord, Height of Body, 9 inches.

THE PAIRPOINT CORPORATION.
NEW BEDFORD, MASS.
38 Murray Street, New York City.
Temple Building, Montreal, Canada.
220 Sutter Street, San Francisco, Cal.
NEG. 288 A

Less Shade, Plain, Old Brass or Jap. Bronze,   8.50
"   "   Engraved,   "   "   "   10.00
No. 966. 8 inch Vienna Shade,   5.00

QUADRUPLE PLATE.

TRADE M

Plate 493. Vienna shade. *Pond lily* decoration #966. Base #3029 1//2. 1900-1903.

No. 3033. ELECTROLIER, with 8 Feet of Silk Cord, Height of Body, 12 inches.

THE PAIRPOINT CORPORATION.
NEW BEDFORD, MASS.
38 Murray Street, New York City.
Temple Building, Montreal, Canada.
220 Sutter Street, San Francisco, Cal.
NEG. 289 A

Less Shade, Plain, Old Brass or Jap. Bronze,
" " Engraved, " " "
" " Plain, Silver,
" " Engraved, Silver,
" " Plain, Gold,
" " Engraved, Gold,
No. 970. 10 inch Vienna Shade,
QUADRUPLE PLATE.

13.00
15.00

9.00 *Even frosted*

TRADE

Plate 494. Vienna shade. *Chrysanthemums* decoration #970. Base #3033. 1900-1903.

Plate 495. Vienna shade. *Ivy leaves* decoration #1334. Base #3047. 1900-1903.

Plate 492. Vienna shade. *Raspberries and spider* decoration #967. #3028 1/2. 1900-1903.

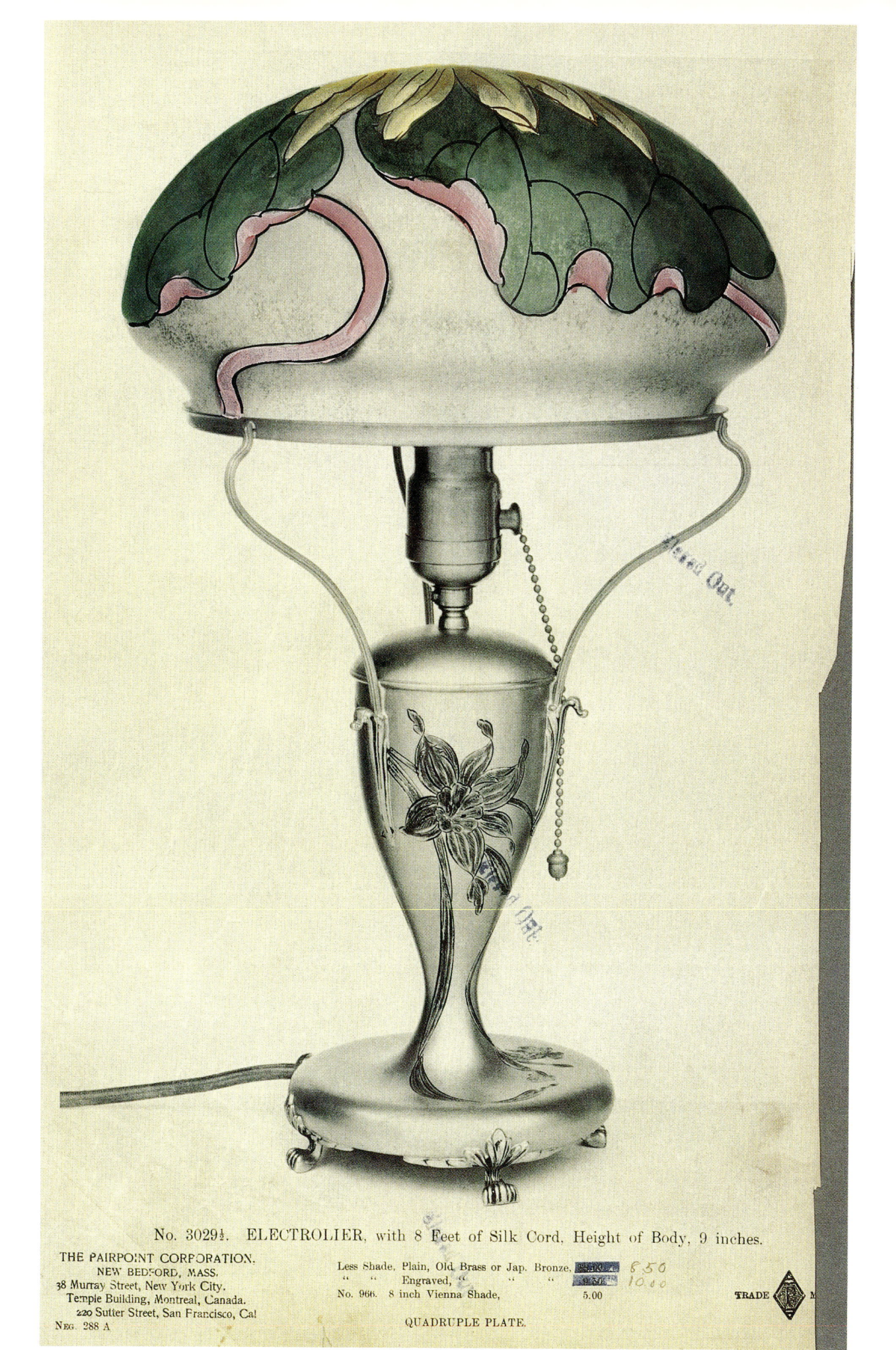

No. 3029½. ELECTROLIER, with 8 Feet of Silk Cord, Height of Body, 9 inches.

THE PAIRPOINT CORPORATION.
NEW BEDFORD, MASS.
38 Murray Street, New York City.
Temple Building, Montreal, Canada.
220 Sutter Street, San Francisco, Cal.
NEG. 288 A

Less Shade, Plain, Old Brass or Jap. Bronze   8.50
   "   "   Engraved,   "   "   "   10.00
No. 966. 8 inch Vienna Shade,   5.00

QUADRUPLE PLATE.

Plate 493. Vienna shade. *Pond lily* decoration #966. Base #3029 1//2. 1900-1903.

No. 3033. ELECTROLIER, with 8 Feet of Silk Cord, Height of Body, 12 inches.

THE PAIRPOINT CORPORATION.
NEW BEDFORD, MASS.
38 Murray Street, New York City.
Temple Building, Montreal, Canada.
220 Sutter Street, San Francisco, Cal.
NEG. 289 A

Less Shade, Plain, Old Brass or Jap. Bronze,
" " Engraved, "
" " Plain, Silver,
" " Engraved, Silver,
" " Plain, Gold,
" " Engraved, Gold,
No. 970. 10 inch Vienna Shade,
QUADRUPLE PLATE.

TRADE

Plate 494. Vienna shade. *Chrysanthemums* decoration #970. Base #3033. 1900-1903.

Plate 495. Vienna shade. *Ivy leaves* decoration #1334. Base #3047. 1900-1903.

No. 3051. ELECTROLIER, with 8 Feet Silk Cord. Height of Body, 8½ inches.

THE PAIRPOINT CORPORATION,
NEW BEDFORD, MASS.
38 Murray Street, New York City.
Temple Building, Montreal, Canada.
220 Sutter Street, San Francisco, Cal.
NEG. 302 A

Less Shade, Old Brass, Green, ~~4.50~~ 10.50
~~No. 1510. 8 inch Vienna Shade, 4.50~~

QUADRUPLE PLATE.

Shade Closed

Copy

TRADE

Plate 496. Vienna shade. *Scroll* decoration #1510. Base #3051. 1900-1903.

Plate 497. Vienna shade. *Bearded iris* decoration #1545. Base #3047. 1904-1906.

No. B 3003.   ELECTROLIER, with 8 Feet Silk Cord, Height of Body, 15 inches.

THE PAIRPOINT CORPORATION.
NEW BEDFORD, MASS.
38 Murray Street, New York City.
36 St. Antoine St., Montreal, Canada.
717 Market St., San Francisco, Cal.
Neg. 471 A

Less Shade, Old Brass, $16.00
    "   "   Two Lights, 20.00
No. 1375.   14 inch Vienna Shade, $16.00

Plate 498. Vienna shade. *Flemish daffodil* decoration #1375. Base #B3003. 1907.

No. B 3001. ELECTROLIER, with 8 Feet Silk Cord, Height of Body, 14 inches.

THE PAIRPOINT CORPORATION.
NEW BEDFORD, MASS.
38 Murray Street, New York City.
36 St. Antoine St., Montreal, Canada.
717 Market St., San Francisco, Cal.
NEG. 472 A

Less Shade, Old Brass, $14.00
" " Double Light, 18.00
No. 1374. 14 inch Vienna Shade. 16.00

Plate 499. Vienna shade. *Window panes* decoration #1374. Base #B3001. 1907.

No. 3009½. ELECTROLIER, with 8 Feet Silk Cord, Height of Body, 8 inches.

THE PAIRPOINT CORPORATION.
NEW BEDFORD, MASS.
38 Murray Street, New York City.
36 St. Antoine St., Montreal, Canada.
717 Market St., San Francisco, Cal.
NEG. 530 A

Less Shade, Old Brass, $8.50
"   "   Two Light, 12.50
No. 1366. 10 inch Vienna Shade, 10.00

TRADE P MARK

Plate 500. Vienna shade. *Flemish maple leaf* decoration #1366. Base #3009 1/2. 1907.

No. C 3058.   ELECTROLIER, with 8 Feet Silk Cord, Height of Body, 8 inches.

Plain, One Light, Less Shade, Old Brass Green, Antique or Gun Metal, $6.85

THE PAIRPOINT CORPORATION,
NEW BEDFORD, MASS.

No. 749. 8 inch Vienna Shade, $5.50

38 Murray Street, New York City.
Coristine Building, St. Nicholas St.,
Montreal, Canada.
717 Market St., San Francisco, Cal.
N eg. 531

TRADE MARK.

Plate 501. Vienna shade. *Cornucopia and ribbon* decoration #749. Base #C3058. 1910-1914.

Shade Closed Out

No. 3037. ELECTROLIER, with 8 Feet Silk Cord, Height of Body, 12 inches.

THE PAIRPOINT CORPORATION,
NEW BEDFORD, MASS.
38 Murray Street, New York City.
36 St. Antoine St., Montreal, Canada.
717 Market St., San Francisco, Cal.
Neg. 531 A

Less Shade, Plain, Old Brass or Jap. Bronze, $12.50
" Engraved, " " " 13.50
With Two Lights, $4.00 extra.
~~No. 1350. 10 inch Vienna Shade, $11.00~~

TRADE MARK

Plate 502. Vienna shade. *Nouveau lilies* decoration #1350. Base #3037. 1907.

No. 3047½. ELECTROLIER, with 8 Feet Silk Cord, Height of Body, 8 inches.

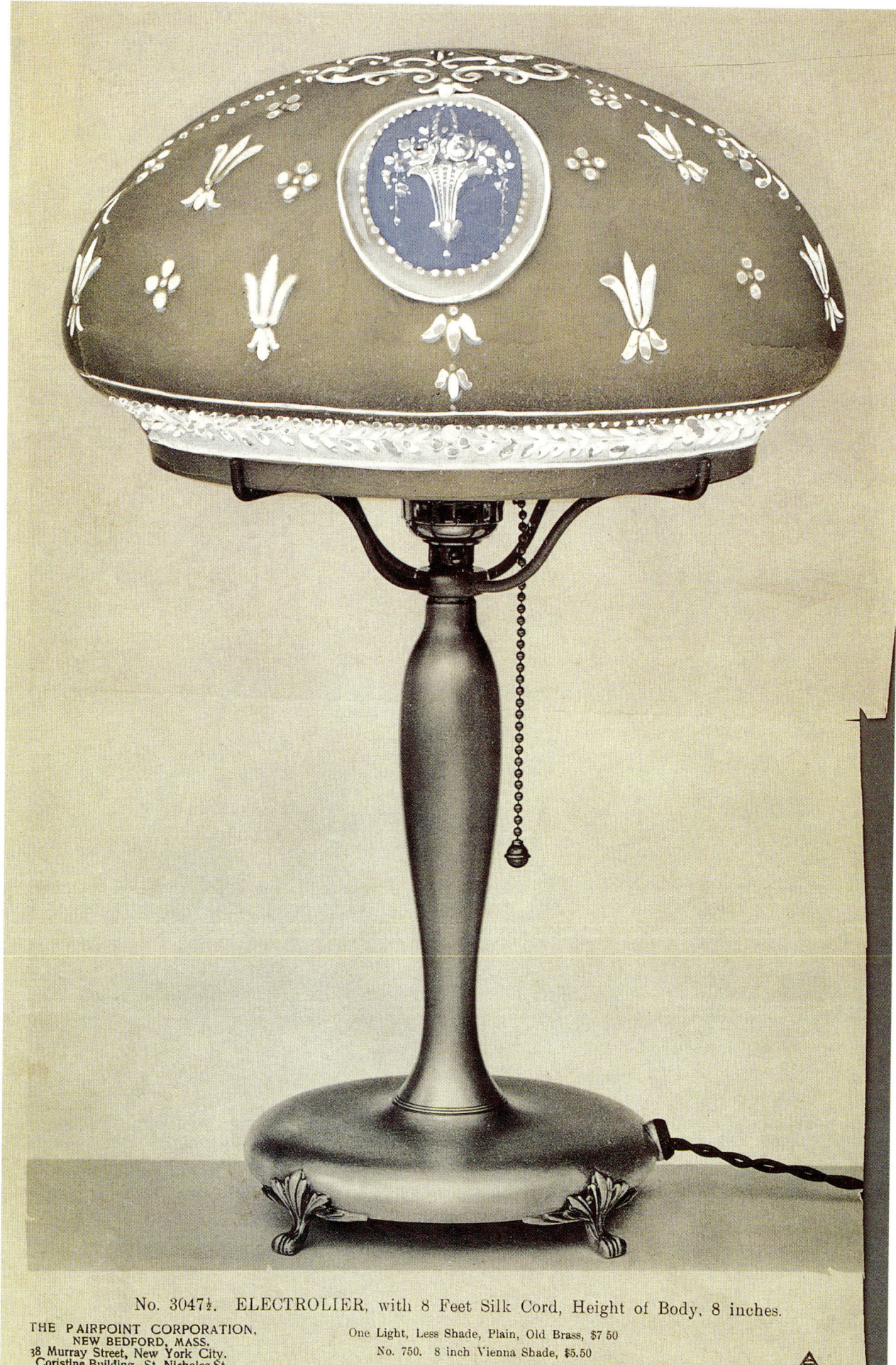

THE PAIRPOINT CORPORATION,
NEW BEDFORD, MASS.
38 Murray Street, New York City.
Coristine Building, St. Nicholas St.,
Montreal, Canada.
717 Market St., San Francisco, Cal.
NEG. 532

One Light, Less Shade, Plain, Old Brass, $7.50
No. 750. 8 inch Vienna Shade, $5.50

TRADE MARK

Plate 503. Vienna shade. *Jasper basket medallion* decoration #750. Base #3047 1/2. 1910-1914.

No. C 3051. ELECTROLIER, with 8 Feet Silk Cord, Height of Body, 9 inches.

One Light, Less Shade, Plain, Old Brass, Antique or Gun Metal, $10.00

No. 751. 8 inch Vienna Shade, $5.00

THE PAIRPOINT CORPORATION,
NEW BEDFORD, MASS.
38 Murray Street, New York City.
Coristine Building, St. Nicholas St.,
Montreal, Canada.
717 Market St., San Francisco, Cal.

NEG. 533

TRADE P MARK.

Plate 504. Vienna shade. *Green leather with rosebuds* decoration #751. Base #C3051. 1910-1914.

No. 3051. ELECTROLIER, with 8 Feet Silk Cord, Height of Body, 8½ inches.

THE PAIRPOINT CORPORATION.
NEW BEDFORD, MASS.
38 Murray Street, New York City.
36 St. Antoine St., Montreal, Canada.
717 Market St., San Francisco, Cal.

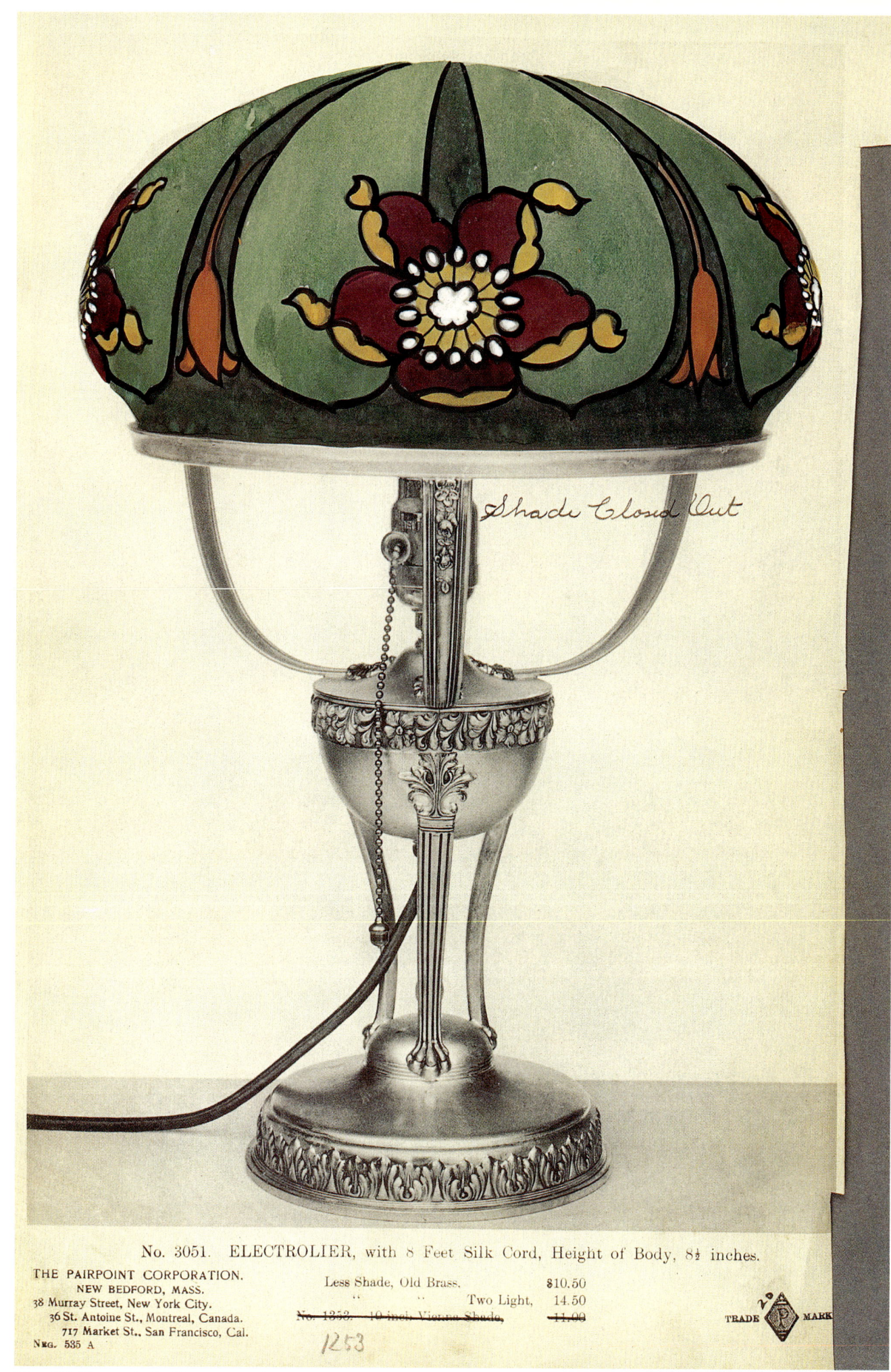

Less Shade, Old Brass. $10.50
"   "   Two Light, 14.50

Plate 505. Vienna shade. *Nouveau rose* decoration #1253. Base 3051. 1907.

No. 3086.   ELECTROLIER, with 8 Feet Silk Cord. Height of Body, 12½ inches.

THE PAIRPOINT CORPORATION,
NEW BEDFORD, MASS.
38 Murray Street, New York City.
36 St. Antoine St., Montreal, Canada.
717 Market St., San Francisco, Cal.

NEG. 543 A

Less Shade, Old Brass, $11.00
"   "   Two Lights,   15.00
No. 1389. 14 inch Vienna Shade,   18.00

Shade Closed Out

Plate 506. Vienna shade. *Torch with floral garland* decoration #1389. Base #3086. 1907.

No. C 3066.   ELECTROLIER.   With 8 Feet Silk Cord, Height of Body, 13 inches.
Special Two Light Fixture, Less Shade, Old Brass Green, Antique or Gun Metal, $10.45

THE PAIRPOINT CORPORATION,
NEW BEDFORD, MASS.
38 Murray Street, New York City.
Coristine Building, St. Nicholas St.,
Montreal, Canada.
717 Market St., San Francisco, Cal.
Neg. 593

No. 710. 14 inch Vienna Shade, $12.75

TRADE MARK

Plate 507. Vienna shade. *Floral bouquet with lattice* decoration #710 (open top). Base #C3066. 1910-1914.

No. 3083. ELECTROLIER, with 8 Feet Silk Cord, Height of Body, 13 inches.

THE PAIRPOINT CORPORATION
NEW BEDFORD, MASS.
38 Murray Street, New York City.
485 St. Catherine St., Montreal, Canada.
717 Market St., San Francisco, Cal.
NEG 732 A

Less Shade, Engraved, Old Brass, $12.00
"   "   "   " Two Lights. 16.00
No. 966. 10 inch Vienna Shade, $7.00

COPY.

Plate 508. Vienna shade. *Nouveau pond lily* decoration #966. Base #3083. 1907-1910.

No. C 3038. PIANO ELECTROLIER, with 8 Feet Silk Cord. Height of Body, 13½ inches.
Two Lights, Less Shade, Plain, Old Brass, Antique or Gun Metal, $12.75
" " Engraved, " Green " " 14.55

THE PAIRPOINT CORPORATION,
NEW BEDFORD, MASS.
38 Murray Street, New York City.
Coristine Building, St. Nicholas St.,
Montreal, Canada.
717 Market St., San Francisco, Cal.
NEG. 392

Fancy Coloring, $ .95 Extra.

No. 1252. 10 inch Wagner Shade, $6.40

TRADE MA[RK]

Plate 509. Wagner shade. Piano lamp. *Poppy tapestry* decoration #1252. Base #C3038. 1910-1914.

No. C 3039. PIANO ELECTROLIER, with 8 Feet Silk Cord. Height of Body, 13½ inches.

Two Lights, Less Shade, Plain, Old Brass, Antique or Gun Metal, $14.55
" " Engraved, " Green " " 16.40

Fancy Coloring, $ .95 Extra.

THE PAIRPOINT CORPORATION,
NEW BEDFORD, MASS.
38 Murray Street, New York City.
Coristine Building, St. Nicholas St.,
Montreal, Canada.
717 Market St., San Francisco, Cal.
NEG. 393

No. 520. 10 inch Wagner Shade, $6 85

TRADE MARK

Plate 510. Wagner shade. Piano lamp. *Evening landscape* decoration #520. Base #C3039. 1910-1914.

No. 3055. ELECTROLIER, with 8 Feet Silk Cord. Height of Body, 11 inches.

THE PAIRPOINT CORPORATION,
NEW BEDFORD, MASS.
38 Murray Street, New York City.
Temple Building, Montreal, Canada.
220 Sutter Street, San Francisco, Cal.

Less Shade, Old Brass, Green,
No. 1538. 10-inch Wakefield Shade,
QUADRUPLE PLATE.

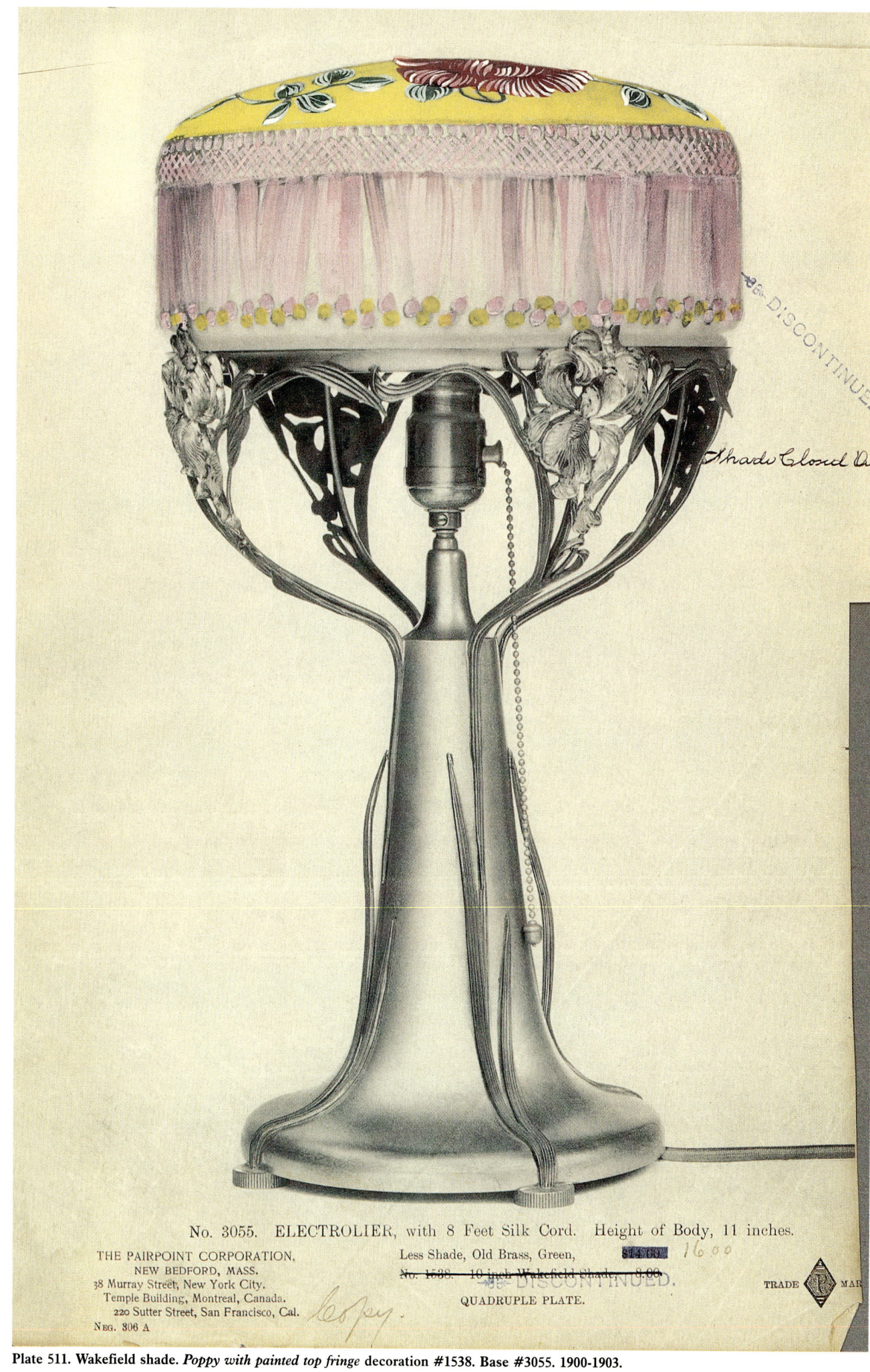

NEG. 306 A

Plate 511. Wakefield shade. *Poppy with painted top fringe* decoration #1538. Base #3055. 1900-1903.

No. 3060. ELECTROLIER, with 8 Feet Silk Cord. Height of Body, 12 inches.

THE PAIRPOINT CORPORATION,
NEW BEDFORD, MASS.
38 Murray Street, New York City.
Temple Building, Montreal, Canada.
220 Sutter Street, San Francisco, Cal.
NEG. 311 A

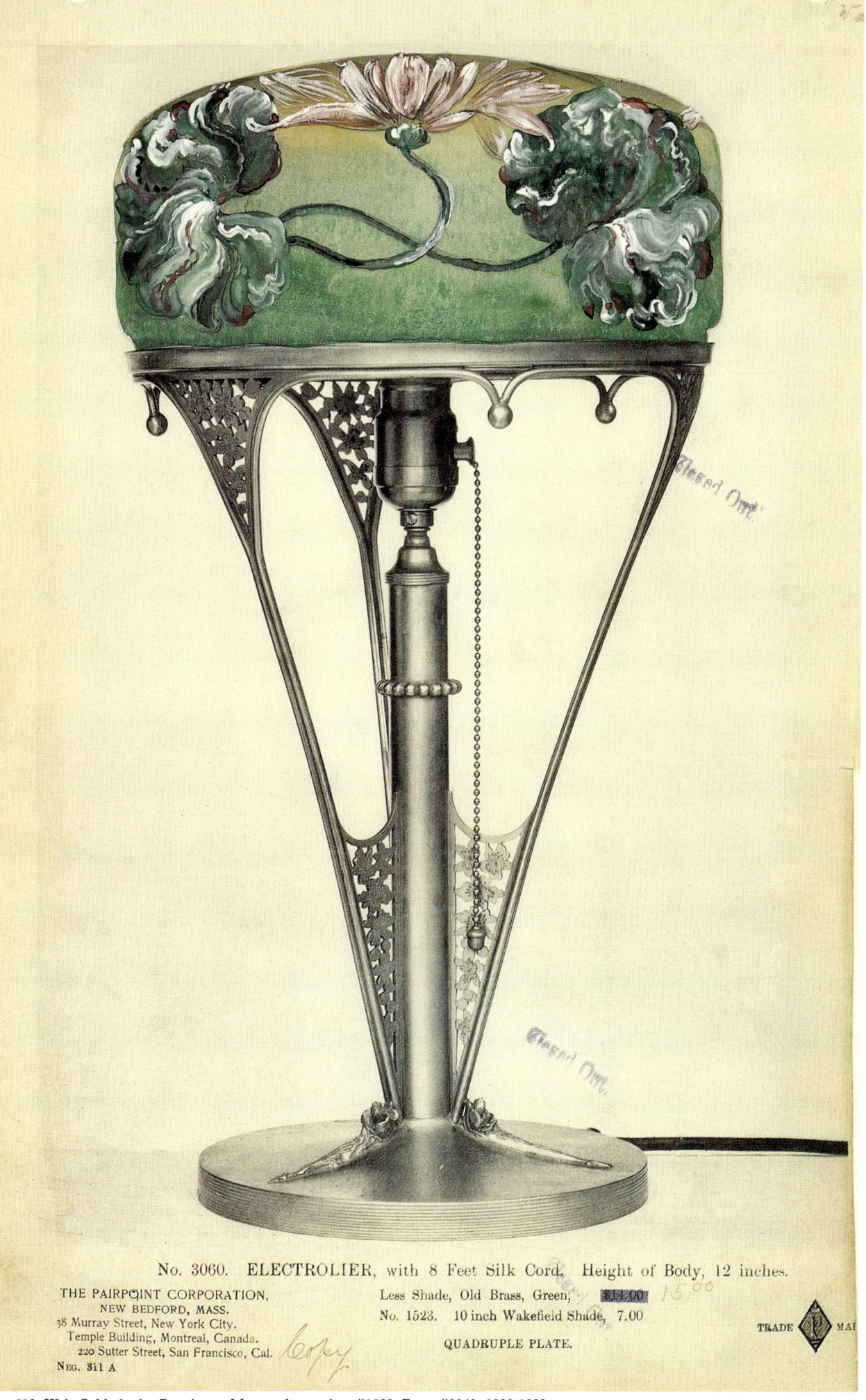

Less Shade, Old Brass, Green, $14.00 15.00
No. 1523. 10 inch Wakefield Shade, 7.00
QUADRUPLE PLATE.

Plate 512. Wakefield shade. *Poppies and leaves* decoration #1523. Base #3060. 1900-1903.

Plate 513. Windsor shade. *Rose on frosted background* decoration #939; Warwick shade. *Turkish carpet* decoration #1341; Balmoral shades. *Butterfly on yellow* decoration #1719; *Butterfly on white* decoration #1715. 1907-1910.

THE PAIRPOINT CORPORATION,
NEW BEDFORD, MASS.
38 Murray Street, New York City.
485 St. Catherine St. Montreal, Canada.
717 Market St. San Francisco, Cal.

NED. 666 A

No. 3078. Less Shade, Old Brass, $4.50
Height of Body, 6½ inches.
No. 1345. 5 inch Worwick Shade, $2.50

No. 3079. Less Shade, Old Brass, $5.00
Height of Body, 7½ inches.
No. 1716. 5 inch Balmoral Shade, $3.00

No. 3080. Less Shade, Old Brass, $5.50
Height of Body, 8½ inches.
No. 938. 5 inch Windsor Shade, $3.00

ELECTROLIERS, with 8 Feet Silk Cord.

Plate 514. Worwick [Warw] shade. *Violets and daisies* decoration #1345. Base #3078; Balmoral shade. *Butterfly and daisy* decoration #1716. Base #3079; Windsor shade. *Pink background with rose* decoration #938. Base #3080. 1907-1910.

Related Materials Electric Candles with Parchment Shades

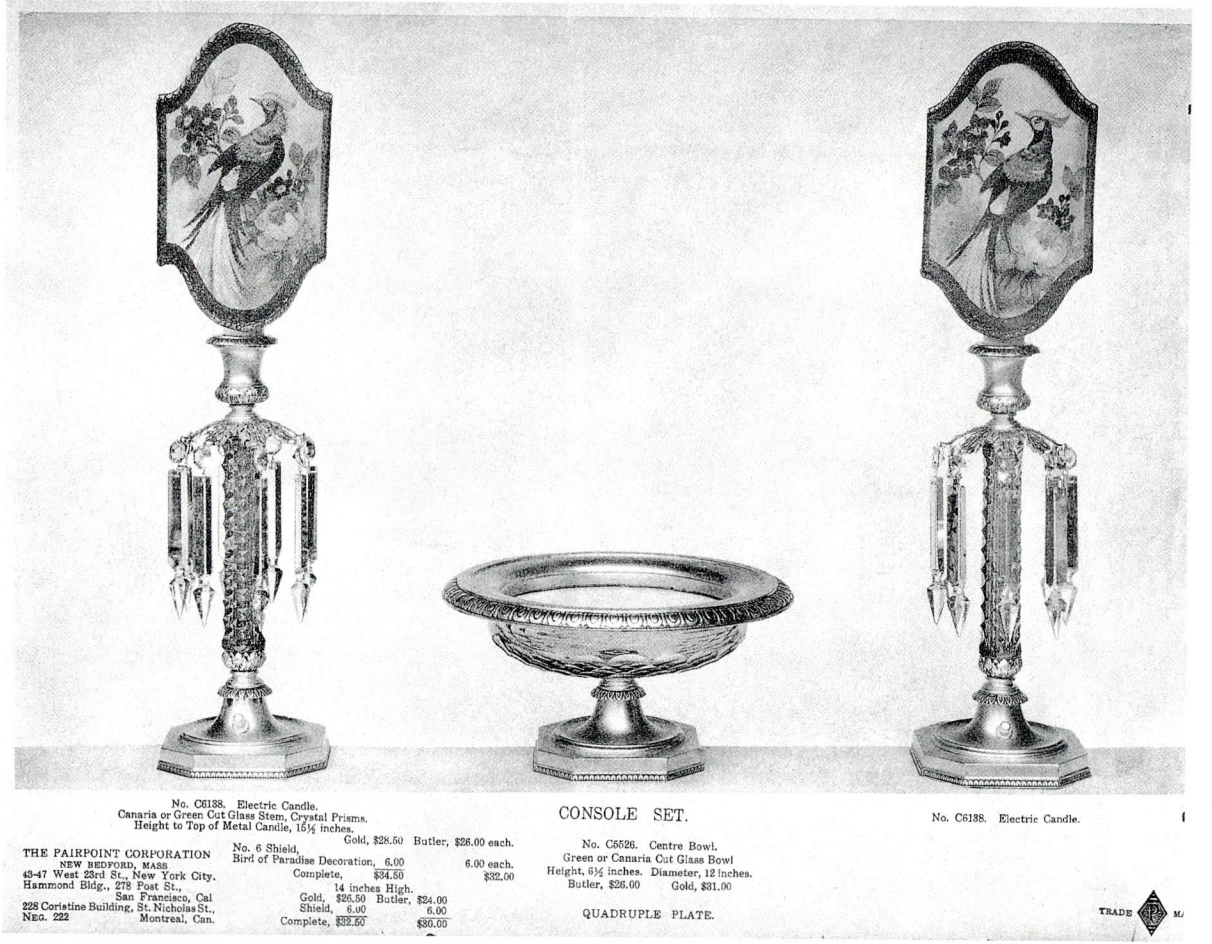

Above: Plate 515. Electric Candles. Shield shade (parchment). Bird of Paradise decoration #6. Base #C6138 (cut glass stem with crystal prisms). Console set, centre bowl #C5526. 1926-1930.

Below: Plate 516. Electric Candles. Shield shade (parchment with Coralene beads). Bird of Paradise decoration #6. Base #C6138 (cut glass stem with crystal prisms); Console set, centre bowl. #C5526. 1926-1930.

6153. ELECTRIC CANDLE.

THE PAIRPOINT CORPORATION
NEW BEDFORD, MASS.
43-47 West 23rd St., New York City.
Hammond Bldg., 278 Post St.,
San Francisco, Cal.
228 Coristine Building, St. Nicholas St.,
NEG. 270   Montreal, Can.

Hei... ...p of Candle Socket, 8½ inches. Marble Base.
Egy... ...ss, Amethyst or Amber Prisms, $16.00
But... ...or Blue Prisms,
No. ...Ship Decoration,   3.50
Complete, $19.50
153½ Fitted for Wax Candle, $13.00
QUADRUPLE PLATE

TRADE MARK

Plate 517. Electric Candle. Shield shade (parchment with Coralene beads). Ship decoration #3. (no #). Base #C6153. 1926-1930.

Coralene Parchment

THE PAIRPOINT CORPORATION
NEW BEDFORD, MASS.
43-47 West 23rd St., New York City.
Hammond Bldg., 278 Post St., San Francisco, Cal.
228 Corinne Building, St. Nicholas St., Montreal, Can.

No. C6147. Electric Candle.
Green or Canaria Cut Glass Stem.
Height to Top of Metal Candle Socket, 9 inches.
No. 2 Square Parchment Shield,
Rose or Peony Decoration,
Gold, $8.50 Butler, $7.50
Complete, 1.75 1.75
$10.25 $9.25

CONSOLE SET.
No. C5524. Centrebowl.
Green or Canaria Cut Glass Bowl.
Height, 6½ inches. Diameter, 9½ inches.
Butler Finish, $10.00
Gold Finish, 11.50

No. C6147½ Fitted for Wax Candle.
Butler, $8.25 Gold, $7.25
QUADRUPLE PLATE.

No. C6147. Electric Candle.

TRADE MARK

Plate 518. Electric Candles. Square shades (parchment with Coralene beads). Peony decoration #2. Base #C6147(cut glass stem with crystal prisms); Console set, centre bowl with prisms #C5524. Rose decoration #2. Base #C6147(cut glass stem with crystal prisms). 1926-1930.

THE PAIRPOINT CORPORATION
NEW BEDFORD, MASS.
43-47 West 23rd St., New York City.
Hammond Bldg., 278 Post St., San Francisco, Cal.
228 Coristine Building, St. Nicholas St., Montreal, Can.
Neg. 226

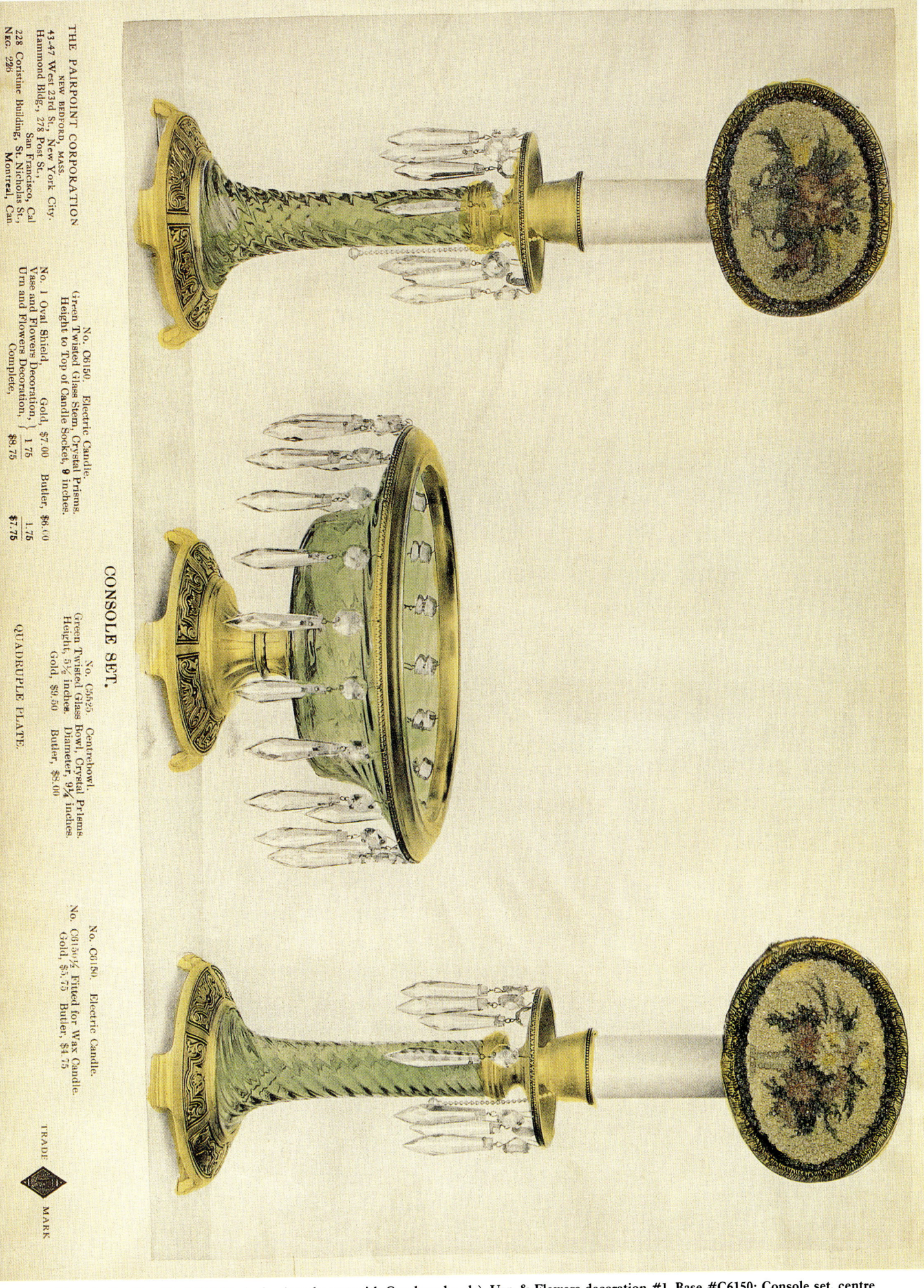

No. C6150. Electric Candle.
Green Twisted Glass Stem, Crystal Prisms.
Height to Top of Candle Socket, 9 inches.
Gold, $7.00   Butler, $6.00
No. 1 Oval Shield, 1.75   1.75
Vase and Flowers Decoration,
Urn and Flowers Decoration,
Complete, $8.75 $7.75

CONSOLE SET.
No. C5525. Centrebowl.
Green Twisted Glass Bowl, Crystal Prisms.
Height, 5½ inches. Diameter, 9¾ inches.
Gold, $9.50   Butler, $8.00
QUADRUPLE PLATE.

No. C6150½. Electric Candle.
Fitted for Wax Candle.
Gold, $5.75   Butler, $4.75

TRADE MARK

Plate 519. Electric Candles. Oval Shield shades (parchment with Coralene beads). Urn & Flowers decoration #1. Base #C6150; Console set, centre bowl with prisms #C5525; Vase and Flowers decoration #1. Base #C6150 (twisted glass pillar with crystal prisms). 1926-1930.

THE PAIRPOINT CORPORATION
NEW BEDFORD, MASS.
43-47 West 23rd St., New York City.
Hammond Bldg., 278 Post St.,
San Francisco, Cal.
228 Coristine Building, St. Nicholas St.
Montreal, Can.
NEG. 249

No. C6152
Height to Top of Metal Socket, 9 inches.
8 in. Empire Parchment Shade,
Blue Bird Decoration,
Complete,
Gold, $14.00   Butler, $12.00
                 6.00   6.00
                $20.00 $18.00
No. C6152½. Fitted for Wax Candle.
Gold, $11.50   Butler, $9.50

ELECTRIC CANDLES.

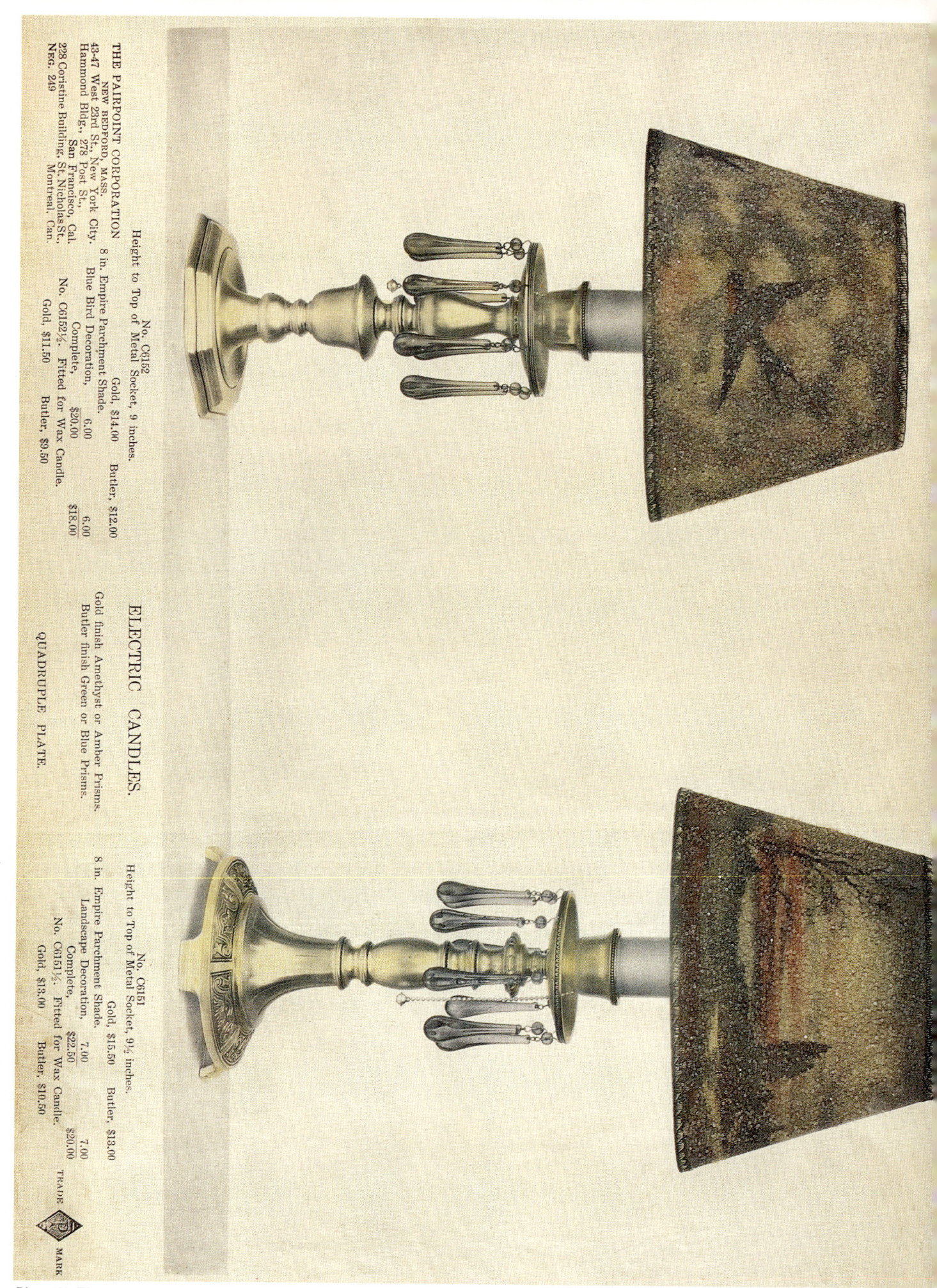

Gold finish Amethyst or Amber Prisms.
Butler finish Green or Blue Prisms.

No. C6151
Height to Top of Metal Socket, 9½ inches.
8 in. Empire Parchment Shade,
Landscape Decoration,
Complete,
Gold, $15.50   Butler, $13.00
       7.00   7.00
      $22.50 $20.00
No. C6151½. Fitted for Wax Candle.
Gold, $13.00   Butler, $10.50

QUADRUPLE PLATE.

TRADE MARK

Plate 520. Electric Candles. Empire Parchment shades (with Coralene beads). Blue Bird decoration no #. Base #C6152. Landscape decoration no #. Base #C6151. 1926-1930.

No. C6153. ELECTRIC CANDLE.

Height to Top of Candle Socket, 8½ inches. Marble Base.
Egyptian Brass, Amethyst or Amber Prisms, } $8.00
Butler, Green or Blue Prisms,
8 in. Empire Parchment Shade, Ship Decoration, 3.50
Complete, $11.50
No. C6153½ Fitted for Wax Candle, $6.50
QUADRUPLE PLATE

THE PAIRPOINT CORPORATION
NEW BEDFORD, MASS.
43-47 West 23rd St., New York City.
Hammond Bldg., 278 Post St.,
San Francisco, Cal
228 Coristine Building, St. Nicholas St.,
NEG. 250   Montreal, Can.

TRADE MARK

Plate 521. Electric Candle. Empire Parchment shade (with Coralene beads). Ship decoration no #. Base #C6153 (with prisms). 1926.

No. C6138.   ELECTRIC CANDLE.   Butler Finish.

Canaria or Green Cut Glass Stem.

THE PAIRPOINT CORPORATION	Height to Top of Metal Candle Socket, 15½ inches, $26.00	14 inches, $24.00
NEW BEDFORD, MASS	8 in. Empire Parchment Shade, Rose Decoration, 8.00	8 in. Shade, 8.00
43-47 West 23rd St., New York City.	Complete, $34.00	$32.00
Hammond Bldg., 278 Post St., San Francisco, Cal	Both Sizes Gold Finish, $2.50 additional.	
228 Coristine Building, St. Nicholas St., Nᴇɢ. 220 Montreal, Can.		

QUADRUPLE PLATE.

TRADE MARK

Plate 522. Electric Candle. Empire Parchment shade (with Coralene beads). Rose decoration no #. Base #C6138 (cut glass stem). No date.

QUADRUPLE PLATE.

No. C6154. ELECTRIC CANDLE.

Height to Top of Candle Socket, 10 inches, Marble Base, Crystal Pendants.
Gold, $10.00   Butler, $9.00

THE PAIRPOINT CORPORATION
NEW BEDFORD, MASS.
43-47 West 23rd St., New York City.
Hammond Bldg., 278 Post St.,
San Francisco, Cal
228 Coristine Building, St. Nicholas St.,
NEG. 268   Montreal, Can.

8 in. Empire Parchment Shade,
Cockatoo Blackground,
   Complete,   4.00   4.00
                              $14.00 $13.00
No. C6154½ Fitted with Wax Candle,
Gold, $8.75   Butler, $7.75

QUADRUPLE PLATE.

TRADE MARK

Plate 523. Electric Candle. Empire Parchment shade (with Coralene beads). Cockatoo, Black background decoration no #. Base #C6154 (with prisms). 1926-1930.

THE PAIRPOINT CORPORATION
NEW BEDFORD, MASS.
43-47 West 23rd St., New York City.
Hammond Bldg., 278 Post St., San Francisco, Cal
228 Coristine Building, St. Nicholas St., Montreal, Can.

ELECTRIC CANDLES.

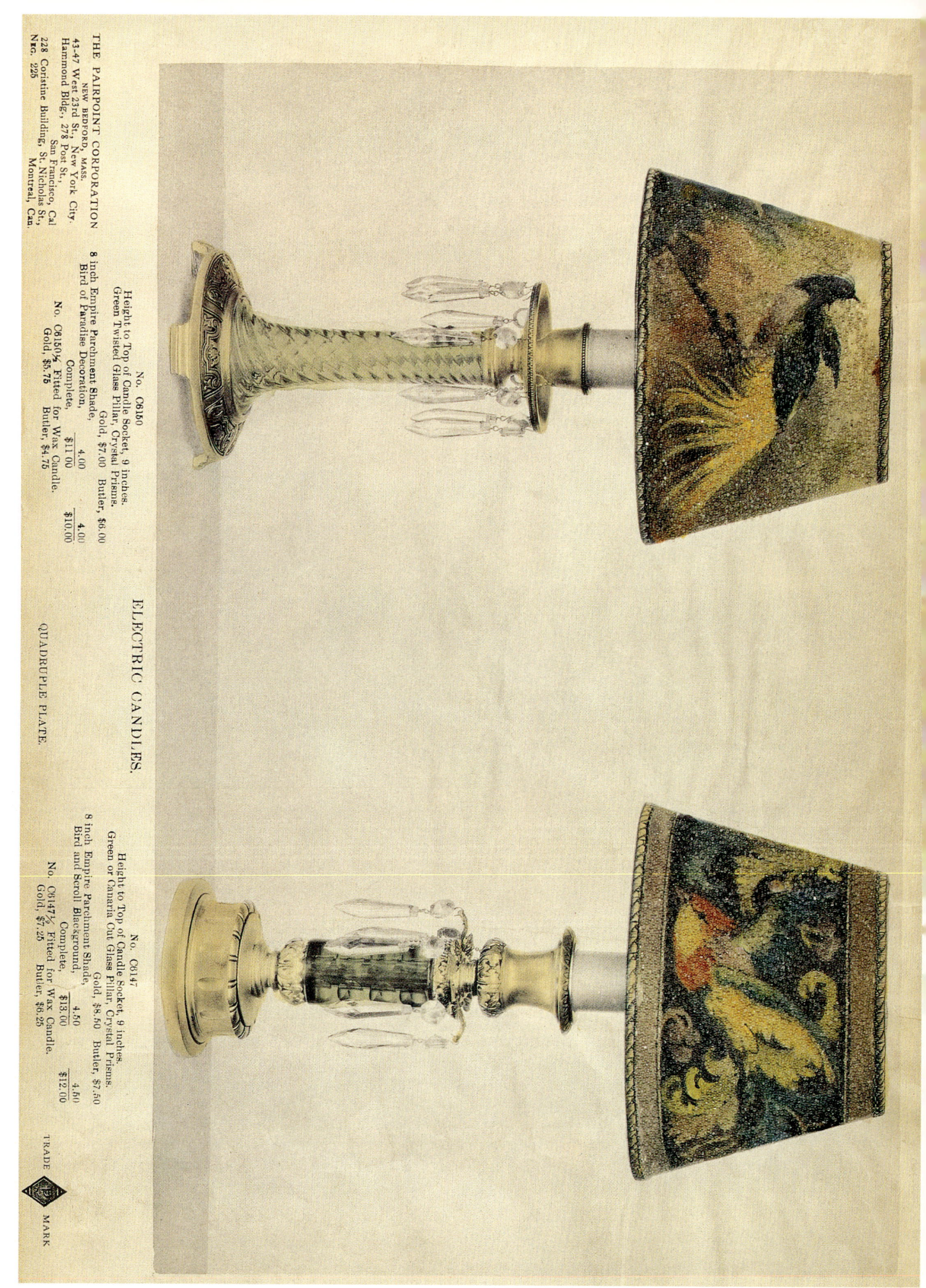

No. C8150
Height to Top of Candle Socket, 9 inches.
Green Twisted Glass Pillar, Crystal Prisms.
Gold, $7.00   Butler, $6.00
8 inch Empire Parchment Shade,
Bird of Paradise Decoration,
Complete,
4.00   4.00
$11.00 $10.00
No. C8150½ Fitted for Wax Candle.
Gold, $5.75   Butler, $4.75

No. C8147
Height to Top of Candle Socket, 9 inches.
Green or Canaria Cut Glass Pillar, Crystal Prisms.
Gold, $8.50   Butler, $7.50
8 inch Empire Parchment Shade,
Bird and Scroll Background,
Complete,
4.50   4.50
$13.00 $12.00
No. C8147½ Fitted for Wax Candle.
Gold, $7.25   Butler, $6.25

QUADRUPLE PLATE.

TRADE MARK

Plate 524. Electric Candles. Empire Parchment shades (with Coralene beads). Bird of Paradise decoration no #. Base #C6150 (twisted glass pillar with crystal prisms); Bird & Scroll, Black background decoration no #. Base #C6147 (cut glass pillar and crystals). 1926-1930.

Color Printed Pages

Base Old Brass, Flemish Brass Bronze and New Antique Finish

Shade Copley Shape No. 449 Narcissus Decoration

Base No.									
Base No.	D 3048	7½ inch	1 Light	$6.85	—10 inch shade	$5.00	Complete	$11.85
"	"	D 3049	12 "	2 "	14.10	—16 "	"	10.00	"	24.10
"	"		12 "	3 "	15.45	—16 "	"	10.00	"	25.45
"	"	D 3050	13½ "	2 "	15.45	—18 "	"	13.10	"	28.55
"	"		13½ "	3 "	16.85	—18 "	"	13.10	"	29.95
"	"	D 3051	15 "	3 "	19.10	—20 "	"	16.90	"	36.00

THE PAIRPOINT CORPORATION, New Bedford, Mass.

New York
43 West 23rd St.

San Francisco
140 Geary St.

Montreal
Coristine Bldg.

Plate 525. Copley shade. Narcissus decoration #449. Base #D3048. 1915-1922.

	Base Solid Mahogany Brass Trimmed					Shade Copley Shape No. 867 Row of Trees Decoration		
Base No.	C 3089	6½ inch	1 Light	$6.40 —	8 inch shade	$4.10	Complete	$10.50
" "	" "	" "	1 "	6.40 — 10	" "	5.90	"	12.30
" "	C 3090	9 "	2 "	9.10 — 12	" "	9.10	"	18.20
" "	" "	" "	2 "	9.10 — 14	" "	11.85	"	20.95
" "	C 3091	12 "	2 "	11.40 — 16	" "	15.45	"	26.85
" "	" "	" "	3 "	12.30 — 18	" "	19.10	"	31.40
" "	C 3092	15 "	3 "	16.40 — 18	" "	19.10	"	35.50
" "	" "	" "	3 "	16.40 — 20	" "	24.55	"	40.95

THE PAIRPOINT CORPORATION, New Bedford, Mass.
SALES ROOMS:

New York	Chicago	Montreal	San Francisco
43 West 23rd St.	402 Columbus Bldg.	Coristine Bldg.	140 Geary St.

Plate 526. Copley shade. Row of Trees decoration #867. Base #C3089 (mahogany). 1915.

Base Solid Mahogany Brass Trimmed								Shade Copley Shape No. 860 Chestnut Decoration		
Base No.	C 3089	6½ inch	1 Light	$6.40	—	8 inch shade	$3.65	Complete	$10.05
"	"	"	"	1 "	6.40	— 10 "	"	5.50	"	11.90
"	C 3090	9 "	2 "	9.10	— 12 "	"	9.10	"	18.20
"	"	9 "	2 "	9.10	— 14 "	"	11.85	"	20.95
"	C 3091	12 "	2 "	11.40	— 16 "	"	14.55	"	25.95
"	"	12 "	3 "	12.30	— 18 "	"	18.20	"	30.50
"	C 3092	15 "	3 "	16.40	— 18 "	"	18.20	"	34.60
"	"	15 "	3 "	16.40	— 20 "	"	21.85	"	38.25

THE PAIRPOINT CORPORATION, New Bedford, Mass.

SALES ROOMS:

New York	Chicago	Montreal	San Francisco
43 West 23rd St.	402 Columbus Bldg.	Coristine Bldg.	140 Geary St.

Plate 527. Copley shade. Chestnut decoration #860. (Ambero). Base #C3089 (mahogany). 1915.

Base Solid Mahogany
Brass Trimmed

Shade Touraine Shape
No. 873 Dresden Decoration

Base No.				Light			8 inch shade		Complete
Base No. C 3093	7 inch	1 Light	$6.40 —	8 inch shade	$6.40	Complete	$12.80
" " " "	" "	1 "	6.40 — 10 "	7.75	"	14.15
" " C 3094	9 "	2 "	9.10 — 12 "	10.00	"	19.10
" " C 3095	12 "	2 "	11.40 — 14 "	11.85	"	23.25
" " " "	" "	2 "	11.40 — 16 "	14.55	"	25.95
" " " "	" "	3 "	12.30 — 16 "	14.55	"	26.85
" " C 3096	15 "	3 "	16.40 — 18 "	20.00	"	36.40

THE PAIRPOINT CORPORATION, New Bedford, Mass.
SALES ROOMS:

New York	Chicago	Montreal	San Francisco
43 West 23rd St.	402 Columbus Bldg.	Coristine Bldg.	140 Geary St.

Plate 528. Touraine shade. Dresden decoration #873. Base #C3093 (mahogany). 1915.

		D3060/302	
	D3060/303		D3060/301
3047½/320			
D3001/307	D3002/308	D3004/309	C6132½/322

Metal Base Old Brass, Flemish Brass, Bronze and New Antique Finishes.

Base No. 3047½ — 12 inch 2 Light $12.30   320 — 14 inch
          Papillon Shade $13.35 Complete 25.65
Base No. 3047½ — 8½ inch 1 Light   6.00   320 — 8 inch
          Papillon Shade 5.35 Complete 11.35
Base No. D3060 Decorations Nos. 301, 302 and 303 Night Lamps
          with wax candle $2.65 with Electric Fittings $4.30

Base No. D3001/307, D3002/308, D3004/309 Boudoir Lamp with
          Electric Fittings $5.00
Base No. C6132½ Mahog. Candle 11 inch $3.65   321, 322 or 323
          9 inch Colonial Shade $3.00 Complete 6.65
Base No. C6132 Mahog. Candle 13 inch   4.30   321, 322 or 323
          9 inch Colonial Shade 3.00 Complete 7.30

Above Night Lamps are with permanent colors, fired. (Mahog. Candle with Elec. Ftgs. $3.35 ex.) (321 Dec. Yellow Butterfly, No. 323 Blue Bird)

THE PAIRPOINT CORPORATION, New Bedford, Mass.

New York: 43 West 23rd Street   San Francisco: 140 Geary Street   Montreal: Coristine Bldg.

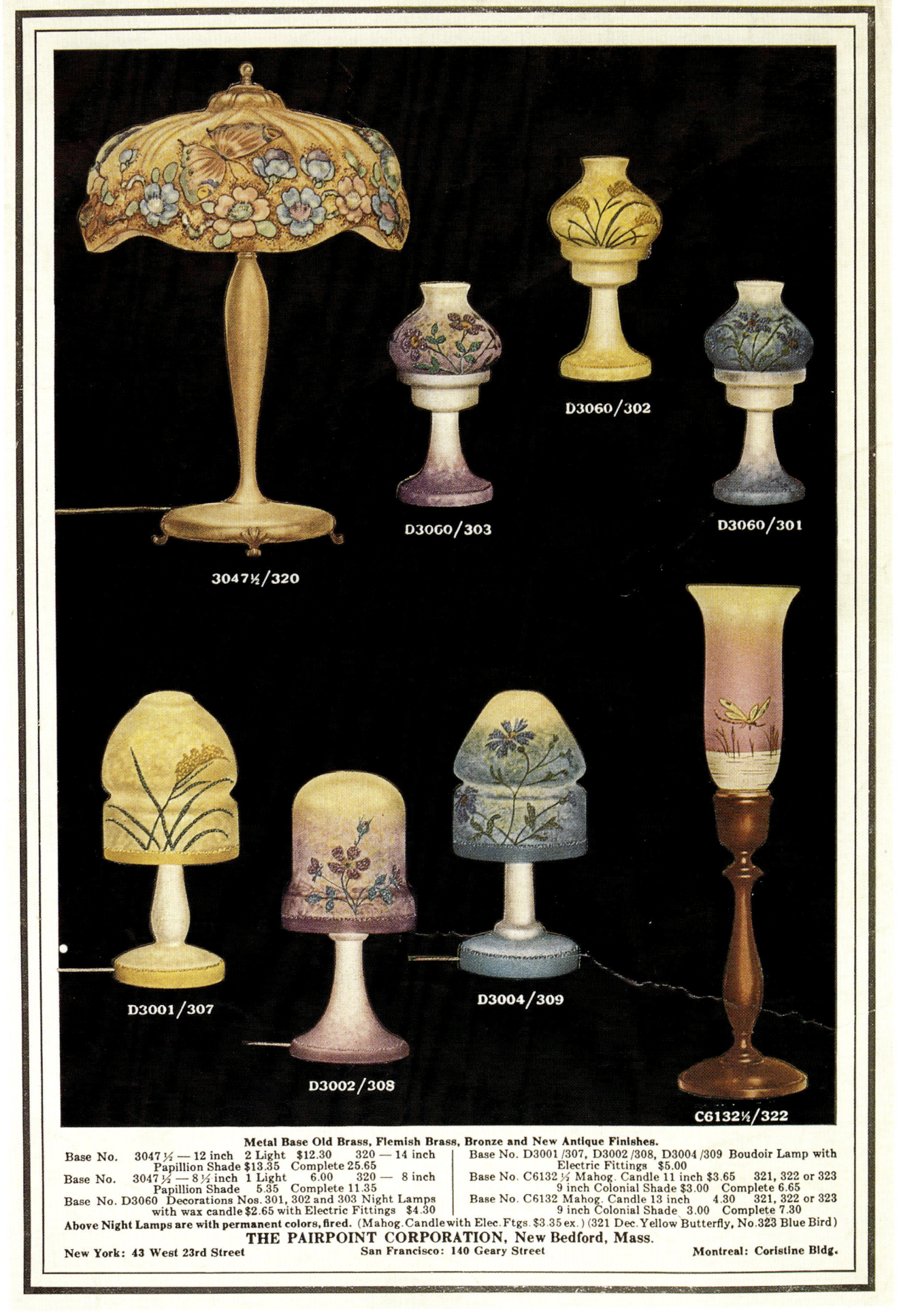

Plate 529 and 530. Top row: Papillon shade. *Floral and butterfly* decoration #320. Base #3047 1/2; Night Lamps. Purple Rose decoration #303. Base #D3060; Goldenrod decoration #302. Base #D3060; Blue bachelor buttons decoration #301. Base #D3060. Bottom row: Boudoir Lamps. Goldenrod decoration #307. Base #D3001; Purple Rose decoration #308. Base #D3002; Blue bachelor buttons decoration #309. Base #D3004; Colonial shade. Dragonfly with pink decoration #322. Base #C6132 1/2 (mahogany candlestick). 1915-1922

**Old Brass, Egyptian Brass,
Flemish, Antique and Bronze Finish**

Base D3071	8 inch	1 Light	$6.00	10 inch Berkley	shade No. 347	$5.30	Complete $11.30
Base D3072	8 inch	1 Light	6.00	8½ inch Lansdowne	shade No. 341	5.35	Complete 11.35
Base D3078	6½ inch	1 Light	8.00	8½ inch Lansdowne	shade No. 348	5.30	Complete 13.30
Base D3073	8 inch	1 Light	6.00	9 inch Carlisle	shade No. 340	4.65	Complete 10.65

THE PAIRPOINT CORPORATION, New Bedford, Mass.

New York
43 West 23d Street

San Francisco
Hammond Building, 278 Post Street

Montreal
Coristine Building

Plate 531. Top row: Lansdowne shade. *Parrot with black background* decoration #341. Base #D3072; Berkley shade. *Blue Birds* decoration #347. Base #D3071; Bottom row: Carlisle shade. *Daisy and butterfly* decoration #340. Base #D3073; Lansdowne shade. *Spanish Galleon* decoration #348. Base #D3078. 1924-1926

D3061/462   C3064/461

D3065/460   3047½/459

Old Brass, Egyptian Brass, Flemish, Antique and Bronze Finish

Base D3061	7½ inch	1 Light	$6.00	8½ inch Bombay shade No. 462	$4.65	Complete	$10.65
Base C3064	7 inch	1 Light	5.45	8½ inch Bombay shade No. 461	4.65	Complete	10.10
Base D3065	8 inch	1 Light	6.00	8½ inch Bombay shade No. 460	5.30	Complete	11.30
Base 3047½	8½ inch	1 Light	6.00	8 inch Stratford shade No. 459	4.00	Complete	10.00

THE PAIRPOINT CORPORATION, New Bedford, Mass.

New York
43 West 23d Street

San Francisco
Hammond Building, 278 Post Street

Montreal
Coristine Building

Plate 532. Top row: Bombay shades. *Green stripe with floral border* decoration #462. Base #D3061; *Stylized Poppy bouquet* decoration #461. Base #C3064. Bottom row: Bombay shade. *Parrot on black background border* decoration #460. Base #D3065; Stratford shade. Puffy. *Green background with flowers* decoration #459. Base #3047 1/2. 1924-1926.

D3072 .345

D3071 344

D3073. 346

D3061. 342

**Old Brass, Egyptian Brass,
Flemish, Antique and Bronze Finish**

Base D3072	8 inch	1 Light $6.00	10 inch Berkley shade No. 345	$5.30	Complete $11.30
Base D3071	8 inch	1 Light 6.00	8½ inch Bombay shade No. 344	5.30	Complete 11.30
Base D3073	8 inch	1 Light 6.00	10 inch Berkley shade No. 346	6.00	Complete 12.00
Base D3061	7½ inch	1 Light 6.00	8 inch Touraine shade No. 342	4.00	Complete 10.00

THE PAIRPOINT CORPORATION, New Bedford, Mass.

New York
43 West 23d Street

San Francisco
Hammond Building, 278 Post Street

Montreal
Coristine Building

Plate 533. Top row: Berkley shade. *Apple blossom with butterfly* decoration #345. Base #D3072; Bombay shade. *Exotic bird* decoration #344. Base #D3071. Bottom row: Berkley shade. *Poppy* decoration #346. Base #D3073; Touraine shade. *Butterfly and iris with pink background* decoration #342. Base #D3061. 1924-1926.

Plate 534. Top row: Lansdowne shade. *Floral with double bands* decoration #466. Base #D3056; Berkley shade. *White floral with green border* decoration #465. Base #D3036. Bottom row: Bombay shade. *Blue urn* decoration #463. Base #C3057; Carlisle shade. *Rose border with leaves* decoration #464. Base #D3040. 1924-1926.

OLD BRASS, EGYPTIAN BRASS, FLEMISH, ANTIQUE AND BRONZE FINISH

Base D3069—12-inch, 3 Light	$13.35
16-inch Bombay Shade, No. 468	14.65
Decoration, Tapestry Landscape	28.00
Base D3069—12-inch, 2 Light	12.00
16-inch Bombay Shade, No. 468	14.65
Decoration, Tapestry Landscape	26.65
Base D3037—12-inch, 3 Light	$17.25
16-inch Bombay Shade, No. 470	13.35
Decoration, Caravels	30.60
Base D3037—12-inch, 2 Light	15.90
16-inch Bombay Shade, No. 470	13.35
Decoration, Caravels	29.25

THE PAIRPOINT CORPORATION, New Bedford, Mass.

New York
43 West 23d Street

San Francisco
Hammond Building, 278 Post Street

Montreal
Coristine Building

Plate 535. Bombay shades. Tapestry landscape decoration #468. Base #D3069; Caravels decoration #470. Base #D3037. 1924-1926

OLD BRASS, EGYPTIAN BRASS, FLEMISH, ANTIQUE AND BRONZE FINISH

Base D3063 — 13-inch, 2 Light	$14.00
18-inch Bombay Shade, No. 338	20.00
Decoration, Birds of Paradise Tapestry	34.00
Base D3063 — 13-inch, 3 Light	$15.35
18-inch Bombay Shade, No. 338	20.00
Decoration, Birds of Paradise Tapestry	35.35
Base D3070 — 13½-inch, 2 Light	$12.70
18-inch Bombay Shade, No. 339	20.00
Decoration, Floral Stripes	32.70
Base D3070 — 13½-inch, 3 Light	$14.00
18-inch Bombay Shade, No. 339	20.00
Decoration, Floral Stripes	34.00

THE PAIRPOINT CORPORATION, New Bedford, Mass.

New York
43 West 23d Street

San Francisco
Hammond Building, 278 Post Street

Montreal
Coristine Building

Plate 536. Bombay shades. Birds of Paradise Tapestry decoration #338. Base #D3063; Floral stripes decoration #339. Base #D3070. No date.

OLD BRASS, EGYPTIAN BRASS, FLEMISH, ANTIQUE AND BRONZE FINISH

Base D3074 — 12-inch, 2 Light.	$12.00
16-inch Bombay Shade, No. 327.	14.65
Decoration, Decorative Landscape.	$26.65
Base D3074 — 12-inch, 3 Light.	$13.35
16-inch Bombay Shade, No. 327.	14.65
Decoration, Decorative Landscape.	$28.00

Base D3074 — 12-inch, 2 Light.	$12.00
16-inch Berkley Shade, No. 329.	10.65
Decoration, Apple Blossoms.	$22.65
Base D3074 — 12-inch, 3 Light.	$13.35
16-inch Berkley Shade, No. 329.	10.65
Decoration, Apple Blossoms.	$24.00

THE PAIRPOINT CORPORATION, New Bedford, Mass.

New York
43 West 23d Street

San Francisco
Hammond Building, 278 Post Street

Montreal
Coristine Building

Plate 537. Bombay shade. Decorative Landscape decoration #327. Base #D3074; Berkley shade. Apple Blossoms decoration #329. Base #D3074. 1924-1926.

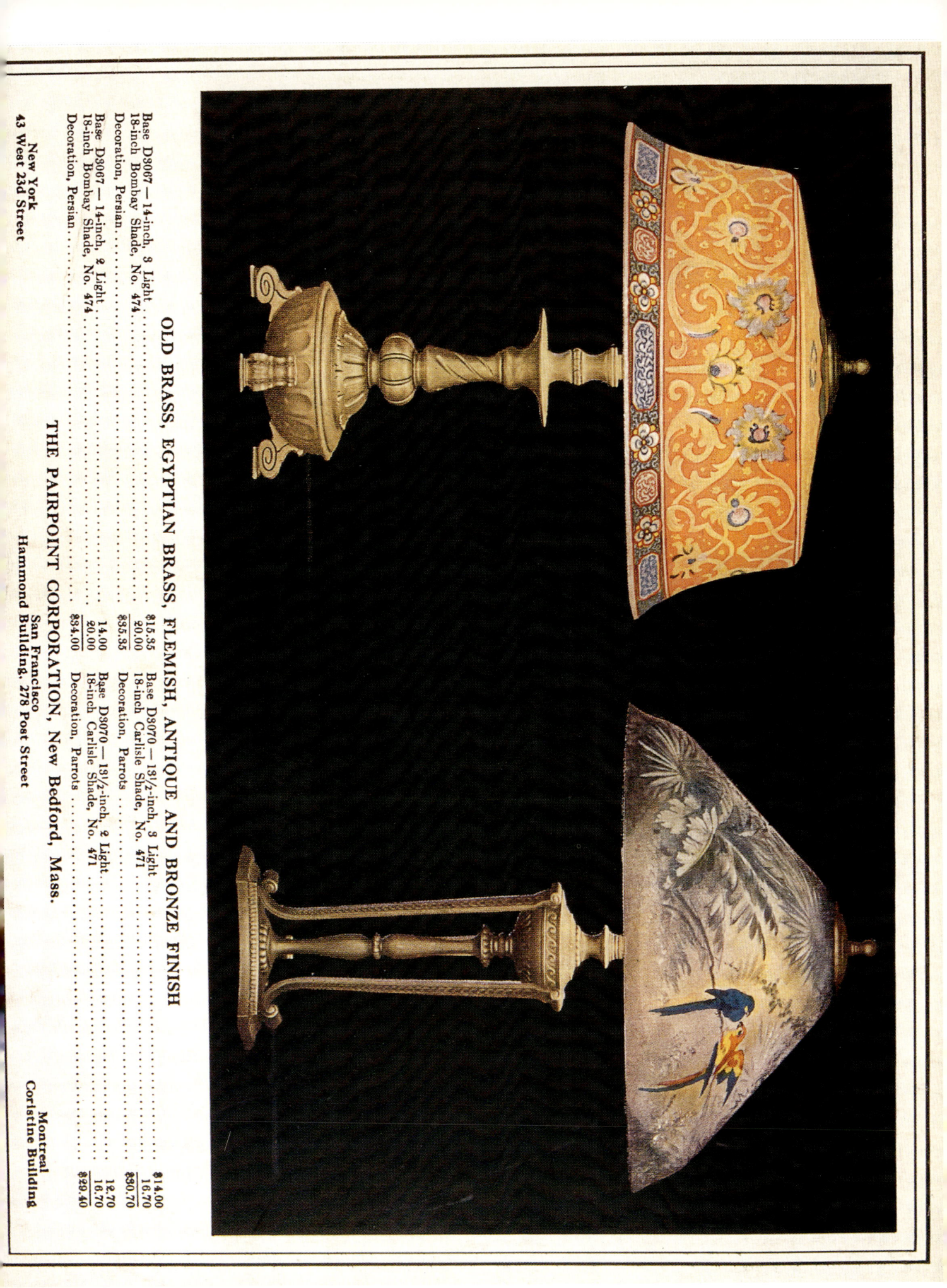

OLD BRASS, EGYPTIAN BRASS, FLEMISH, ANTIQUE AND BRONZE FINISH

Base D3067—14-inch, 3 Light	$15.35
18-inch Bombay Shade, No. 474	20.00
Decoration, Persian	$35.35
Base D3067—14-inch, 2 Light	14.00
18-inch Bombay Shade, No. 474	20.00
Decoration, Persian	$34.00
Base D3070—13½-inch, 3 Light	$14.00
18-inch Carlisle Shade, No. 471	16.70
Decoration, Parrots	$30.70
Base D3070—13½-inch, 2 Light	12.70
18-inch Carlisle Shade, No. 471	16.70
Decoration, Parrots	$29.40

THE PAIRPOINT CORPORATION, New Bedford, Mass.

New York
43 West 23d Street

San Francisco
Hammond Building, 278 Post Street

Montreal
Coristine Building

Plate 538 and 539. Bombay shade. Persian decoration #474. Base #D3067; Carlisle shade. Parrots decoration #471. Base #D3070. 1924-1926.

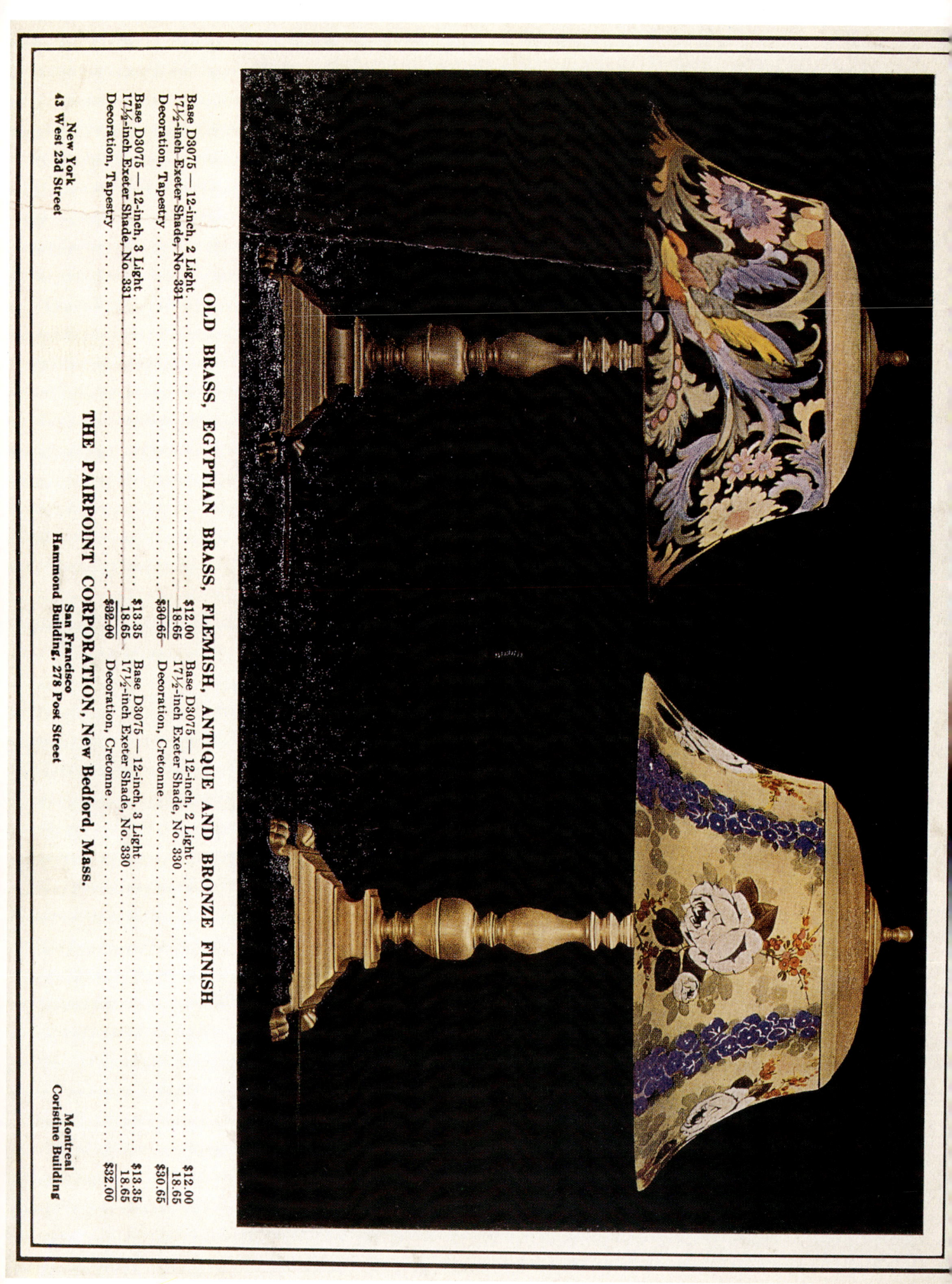

OLD BRASS, EGYPTIAN BRASS, FLEMISH, ANTIQUE AND BRONZE FINISH

Base D3075 — 12-inch, 2 Light	$12.00
17½-inch Exeter Shade, No. 330.	18.65
Decoration, Cretonne	$30.65
Base D3075 — 12-inch, 3 Light	$13.35
17½-inch Exeter Shade, No. 330	18.65
Decoration, Cretonne	$32.00

Base D3075 — 12-inch, 2 Light	$12.00
17½-inch Exeter Shade-No. 331	18.65
Decoration, Tapestry	$30.65
Base D3075 — 12-inch, 3 Light	$13.35
17½-inch Exeter Shade, No. 331	18.65
Decoration, Tapestry	$32.00

THE PAIRPOINT CORPORATION, New Bedford, Mass.

New York
43 West 23d Street

San Francisco
Hammond Building, 278 Post Street

Montreal
Coristine Building

Plate 540. Exeter shades. Tapestry decoration #331. Base #D3075; Cretonne decoration #330. Base #D3075. 1924-1926.

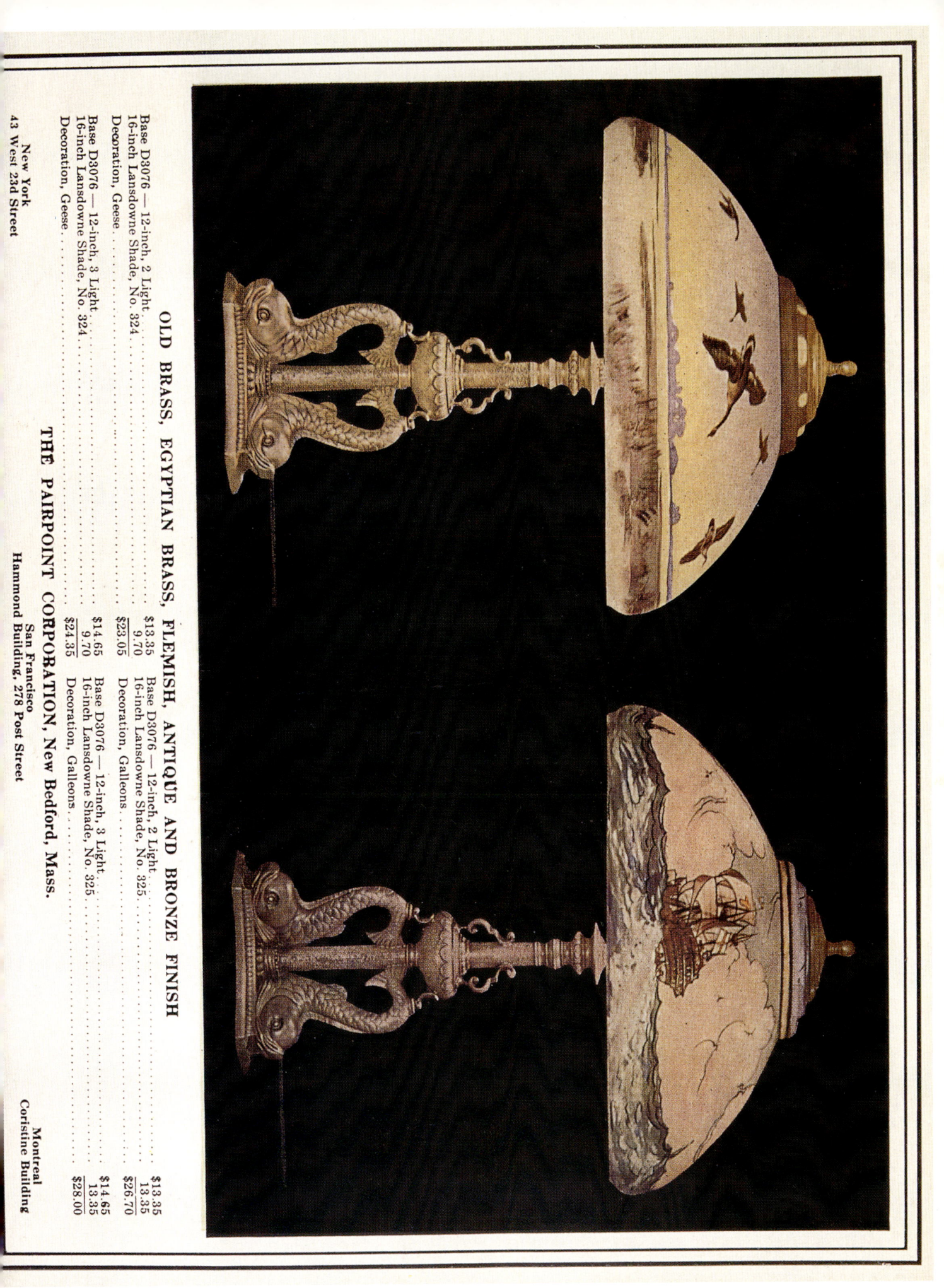

OLD BRASS, EGYPTIAN BRASS, FLEMISH, ANTIQUE AND BRONZE FINISH

Base D3076 — 12-inch, 2 Light	$13.35
16-inch Lansdowne Shade, No. 324	9.70
Decoration, Geese	$23.05
Base D3076 — 12-inch, 3 Light	$14.65
16-inch Lansdowne Shade, No. 324	9.70
Decoration, Geese	$24.35

Base D3076 — 12-inch, 2 Light	$13.35
16-inch Lansdowne Shade, No. 325	13.35
Decoration, Galleons	$26.70
Base D3076 — 12-inch, 3 Light	$14.65
16-inch Lansdowne Shade, No. 325	13.35
Decoration, Galleons	$28.00

THE PAIRPOINT CORPORATION, New Bedford, Mass.

New York
43 West 23d Street

San Francisco
Hammond Building, 278 Post Street

Montreal
Coristine Building

Plate 541. Lansdowne shades. Geese decoration #324. Base #D3076; Galleons decoration #325. Base #D3076. No date.

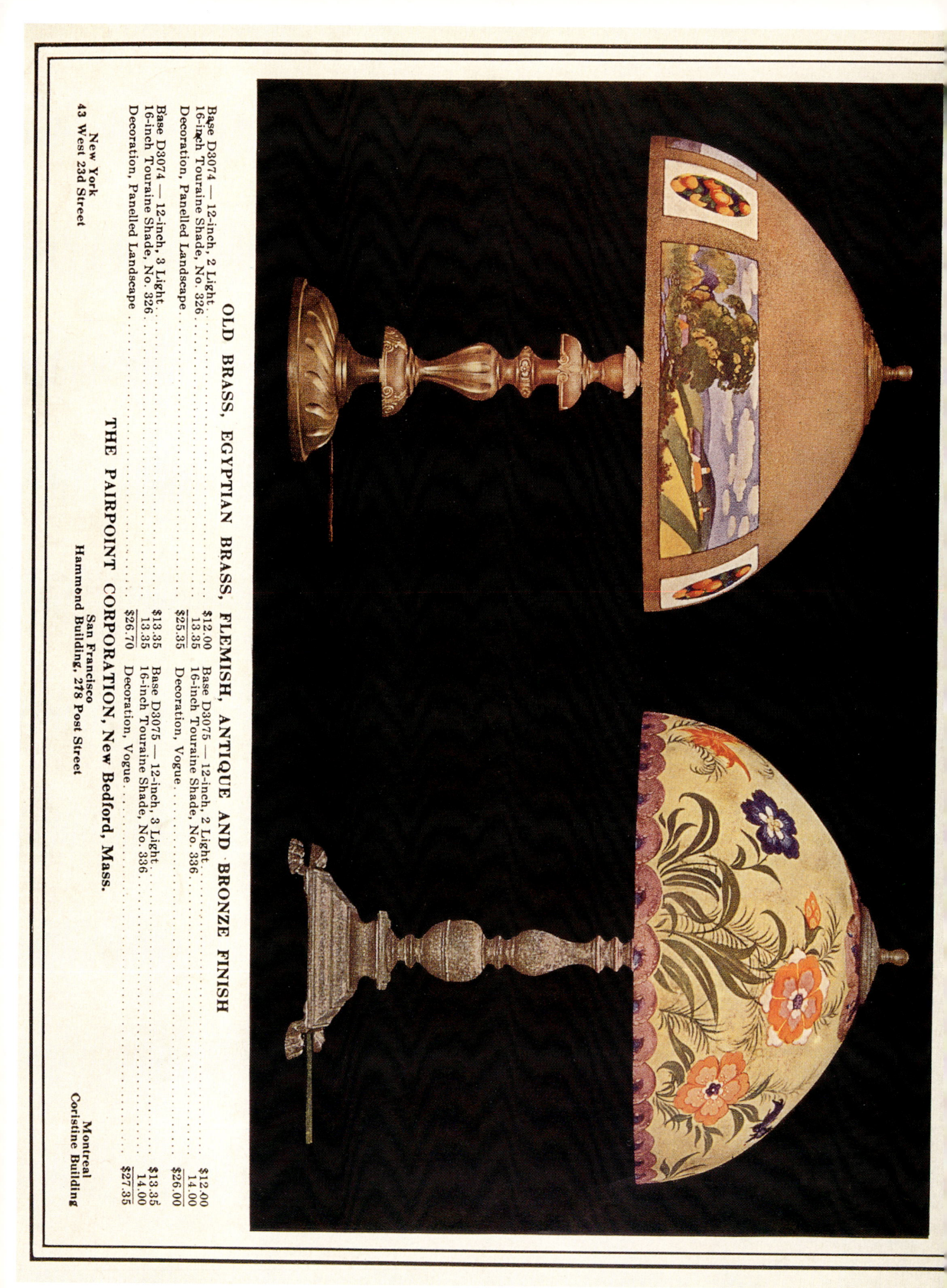

OLD BRASS, EGYPTIAN BRASS, FLEMISH, ANTIQUE AND BRONZE FINISH

Base D3074 — 12-inch, 2 Light	$12.00
16-inch Touraine Shade, No. 326	13.35
Decoration, Panelled Landscape	$25.35
Base D3074 — 12-inch, 3 Light	$13.35
16-inch Touraine Shade, No. 326	13.35
Decoration, Panelled Landscape	$26.70

Base D3075 — 12-inch, 2 Light	$12.00
16-inch Touraine Shade, No. 336	14.00
Decoration, Vogue	$26.00
Base D3075 — 12-inch, 3 Light	$13.35
16-inch Touraine Shade, No. 336	14.00
Decoration, Vogue	$27.35

THE PAIRPOINT CORPORATION, New Bedford, Mass.

New York
43 West 23d Street

San Francisco
Hammond Building, 278 Post Street

Montreal
Coristine Building

Plate 542. Touraine shades. Paneled Landscape decoration #326. Base #D3074; Vogue decoration #336. Base #D3075. 1924-1926.

**Base Old Brass, Flemish Brass
Bronze and New Antique Finish**

**Shade Bombay Shape
No. 444 Italian Landscape Decoration**

Base No.										
Base No.	D 3052	7½ inch	1 Light	$7.50—	8½ inch shade	$6.55	Complete	$14.05
" "	D 3053	12 "	2 "	15.90—	16 " "	17.50	"	33.40
" "	"	12 "	3 "	17.25—	16 " "	17.50	"	34.75
" "	D 3054	13½ "	2 "	18.20—	18 " "	21.25	"	39.45
" "	"	13½ "	3 "	19.55—	18 " "	21.25	"	40.80
" "	D 3055	15 "	3 "	22.75—	20 " "	26.25	"	49.00

THE PAIRPOINT CORPORATION, New Bedford, Mass.

New York
43 West 23rd St.

San Francisco
140 Geary St.

Montreal
Coristine Bldg.

Plate 543. Bombay shade. Italian Landscape decoration #444. Base #D3052. 1915-1922.

**Base Old Brass, Flemish Brass
Bronze and New Antique Finish**

**Shade Bombay Shape
No. 443 Plaza Decoration**

Base No.									
D 3052	7½ inch	1 Light	$7.50—	8½ inch shade	$6.35	Complete	$13.85
" "	D 3053	12 "	2 "	15.90—16	" "	16.90	"	32.80
" "		12 "	3 "	17.25—16	" "	16.90	"	34.15
" "	D 3054	13½ "	2 "	18.20—18	" "	20.00	"	38.20
" "		13½ "	3 "	19.55—18	" "	20.00	"	39.55
" "	D 3055	15 "	3 "	22.75—20	" "	25.00	"	47.75

THE PAIRPOINT CORPORATION, New Bedford, Mass.

New York
43 West 23rd St.

San Francisco
140 Geary St.

Montreal
Coristine Bldg.

Plate 544. Bombay shade. Plaza (Sea lions) decoration #443. Base #D3052. 1915-1922.

Base Old Brass, Flemish Brass, Bronze and New Antique Finish				Shade Bombay Shape No. 452 Moonlight Decoration		
Base No. D3056	7 inch	1 Light	$7.50 — 8½ inch shade	$5.00	Complete	$12.50
" " D3057	12 "	2 "	13.35 — 16 " "	14.65	"	28.00
" " "	12 "	3 "	14.65 — 16 " "	14.65	"	29.30
" " D3058	13 "	2 "	15.35 — 18 " "	16.65	"	32.00
" " "	13 "	3 "	16.65 — 18 " "	16.65	"	33.30
" " D3059	14 "	3 "	19.35 — 20 " "	21.35	"	40.70

THE PAIRPOINT CORPORATION, New Bedford, Mass.

New York: 43 West 23rd St.   San Francisco: 140 Geary St.   Montreal: Coristine Bldg.

Plate 545. Bombay shade. Moonlight (*New Bedford Harbor*) decoration #452. Base #D3056. 1915-1922.

Plate 546. Bombay shade. Berkshire decoration #312. Base #D3061. 1915-1922.

Plate 547. Carlisle shade. Ritz decoration #451. Base #D3017. 1915-1922.

Base Old Brass, Flemish Brass and Bronze Finish			Shade Carlisle Shape No. 429 Old English Tapestry Decoration		
Base No. D3024½ 7½ inch	....	1 Light $7.45—	9 inch shade $5.95	Complete	$13.40
" " " " " "	Silver Plated Butler 1	7.90— 9	" " 5.95		13.85
" " D3025½ 11½ "	....	2 13.20—15	" " 14.55		27.75
" " " " " "	Silver Plated Butler 2	15.00—15	" " 14.55		29.55
" " D3026½ 13½ "	....	2 15.00—18	" " 18.20		33.20
" " " " " "	....	3 16.40—18	" " 18.20		34.60
" " " " " "	Silver Plated Butler 2	17.30—18	" " 18.20		35.50
" " " " " "	" " " 3	18.65—18	" " 18.20		36.85
" " D3027½ 15 "	....	3 18.65—21	" " 23.65		42.30
" " " " " "	Silver Plated Butler 3	21.70—21	" " 23.65		45.35

THE PAIRPOINT CORPORATION, New Bedford, Mass.

New York: 43 West 23rd St.   San Francisco: 140 Geary St.   Montreal: Coristine Bldg.

Plate 548. Carlisle shade. Old English Tapestry decoration #429. Base #D3024 1/2. 1915-1922.

**Base Old Brass, Flemish Brass
Bronze and New Antique Finish**

**Shade Carlisle Shape
No. 448 Vespers Decoration**

Base No.									
D 3048	7½ inch	1 Light	$6.85 —	9 inch shade	$3.75	Complete	$10.60
D 3049	12 "	2 "	14.10 —	15 " "	8.75	"	22.85
"	12 "	3 "	15.45 —	15 " "	8.75	"	24.20
D 3050	13½ "	2 "	15.45 —	18 " "	11.25	"	26.70
"	13½ "	3 "	16.85 —	18 " "	11.25	"	28.10
D 3051	15 "	3 "	19.10 —	21 " "	15.00	"	34.10

THE PAIRPOINT CORPORATION, New Bedford, Mass.

New York
43 West 23rd St.

San Francisco
140 Geary St.

Montreal
Coristine Bldg.

Plate 549. Carlisle shade. Vespers decoration #448. Base #D3048. 1915-1922

Base Old Brass, Flemish Brass
Bronze and New Antique Finish

Shade Carlisle Shape
No. 447 Garden of Allah Decoration

Base No.									
Base No. D 3052	7½ inch	1 Light	$7.50—	9 inch shade	$5.65	Complete	$13.15
" " D 3053	12 "	2 "	15.90—15 "	"	13.75	"	29.65
" " "	12 "	3 "	17.25—15 "	"	13.75	"	31.00
" " D 3054	13½ "	2 "	18.20—18 "	"	17.50	"	35.70
" " "	13½ "	3 "	19.55—18 "	"	17.50	"	37.05
" " D 3055	15 "	3 "	22.75—21 "	"	22.50	"	45.25

THE PAIRPOINT CORPORATION, New Bedford, Mass.

New York
43 West 23rd St.

San Francisco
140 Geary St.

Montreal
Coristine Bldg.

Plate 550. Carlisle shade. Garden of Allah decoration #447. Base #D3052. 1915-1922.

**Old Brass, Egyptian Brass,
Flemish, Antique and Bronze Finish**

**Shade Carlisle Shape
No. 477 Decorations Sand Dunes**

Base D3056	7 inch	1 Light	$7.50 — 9 inch shade $5.00	Complete $12.50
Base D3057	12 inch	2 Light	13.35 — 15 inch shade 10.65	Complete 24.00
Base D3057	12 inch	3 Light	14.65 — 15 inch shade 10.65	Complete 25.30
Base D3058	13 inch	2 Light	15.35 — 18 inch shade 14.70	Complete 30.05
Base D3058	13 inch	3 Light	16.65 — 18 inch shade 14.70	Complete 31.35
Base D3059	14 inch	3 Light	19.35 — 21 inch shade 18.65	Complete 38.00

THE PAIRPOINT CORPORATION, New Bedford, Mass.

New York
43 West 23d Street

San Francisco
Hammond Building, 278 Post Street

Montreal
Coristine Building

Plate 551. Carlisle shade. Sand Dunes decoration #477. Base #D3056. 1924-1926.

Base Old Brass, Flemish Brass, Bronze and New Antique Finish

**Shade Carlisle Shape
No. 313 Canterbury Decoration**

Base No.			Light			inch shade		Complete
D3061	7½ inch	1	Light	$6.00 — 9	inch shade	$4.65		$10.65
D3062	12 "	2	"	12.00 — 15	" "	11.35	"	23.35
D3062	12 "	3	"	13.35 — 15	" "	11.35	"	24.70
D3063	13 "	2	"	14.00 — 18	" "	14.65	"	28.65
D3063	13 "	3	"	15.35 — 18	" "	14.65	"	30.00
D3064	15 "	3	"	17.30 — 21	" "	17.30	"	34.60

THE PAIRPOINT CORPORATION, New Bedford, Mass.

New York:
43 West 23rd Street

San Francisco:
140 Geary Street

Montreal:
Coristine Bldg.

Plate 552. Carlisle shade. Canterbury decoration #313. Base #D3061. 1915-1922.

Plate 553. Copley shade. Maxfield Parrish decoration #866. Base #C3085 (mahogany). 1915.

Base Solid Mahogany Brass Trimmed					Shade Copley Shape No. 861 White Oat-Meal Decoration		
Base No. C 3085	6½ inch	1 Light	$6.40 —	8 inch shade	$3.20	Complete	$9.60
" " "	" "	1 "	6.40 — 10 "	"	4.55	"	10.95
" " C 3086	9 "	2 "	9.10 — 12 "	"	6.85	"	15.95
" " "	" "	2 "	9.10 — 14 "	"	10.00 *8.20*	"	19.10 *17.30*
" " C 3087	12 "	2 "	11.40 — 16 "	"	13.20 *10.60*	"	24.60 *21.40*
" " "	" "	3 "	12.30 — 18 "	"	15.90 *11.85*	"	28.20 *24.15*
" " C 3088	15 "	3 "	16.40 — 18 "	"	15.90 *11.85*	"	32.30 *28.25*
" " "	" "	3 "	16.40 — 20 "	"	19.10 *15.15*	"	35.50 *31.85*

THE PAIRPOINT CORPORATION, New Bedford, Mass.

SALES ROOMS :

New York	Chicago	Montreal	San Francisco
43 West 23rd St.	402 Columbus Bldg.	Coristine Bldg.	140 Geary St.

Plate 554. Copley shade. White Oat-Meal decoration #861. Base #C3085 (mahogany). 1915.

Base Solid Mahogany Brass Trimmed					Shade Copley Shape No. 868 Moonlight Decoration			
Base No.	C 3089	6½ inch	1 Light	$6.40 —	8 inch shade	$3.65	Complete	$10.05
" "	" "	" "	1 "	6.40 — 10	" "	5.50	"	11.90
" "	C 3090	9 "	2 "	9.10 — 12	" "	9.10	"	18.20
" "	" "	" "	2 "	9.10 — 14	" "	11.85	"	20.95
" "	C 3091	12 "	2 "	11.40 — 16	" "	14.55	"	25.95
" "	" "	" "	3 "	12.30 — 18	" "	18.20	"	30.50
" "	C 3092	15 "	3 "	16.40 — 18	" "	18.20	"	34.60
" "	" "	" "	3 "	16.40 — 20	" "	21.85	"	38.25

THE PAIRPOINT CORPORATION, New Bedford, Mass.

SALES ROOMS:

New York	Chicago	Montreal	San Francisco
43 West 23rd St.	402 Columbus Bldg.	Coristine Bldg.	140 Geary St.

Plate 555. Copley shade. Moonlight decoration #868. Base #C3089 (mahogany). 1915.

	Base Solid Mahogany Brass Trimmed					Shade Copley Shape No. 860 Chestnut Decoration			
Base No.	C 3089	6½ inch	1 Light	$6.40 —	8 inch shade	$3.65	Complete	$10.05
"	"	"	1 "	6.40 — 10	" "	5.50	"	11.90
"	C 3090	9 "	2 "	9.10 — 12	" "	9.10	"	18.20
"	"	"	2 "	9.10 — 14	" "	11.85	"	20.95
"	C 3091	12 "	2 "	11.40 — 16	" "	14.55	"	25.95
"	"	12 "	3 "	12.30 — 18	" "	18.20	"	30.50
"	C 3092	15 "	3 "	16.40 — 18	" "	18.20	"	34.60
"	"	15 "	3 "	16.40 — 20	" "	21.85	"	38.25

THE PAIRPOINT CORPORATION, New Bedford, Mass.
SALES ROOMS:

New York	Chicago	Montreal	San Francisco
43 West 23rd St.	402 Columbus Bldg.	Coristine Bldg.	140 Geary St.

Plate 556. Copley shade. Chestnut decoration #860 (Ambero). Base #C3089 (mahogany). 1915.

Base Solid Mahogany
Brass Trimmed

Shade Copley Shape
No. 862 Sunset Decoration

Base No.									
C 3093	7 inch	1 Light	$6.40	—	8 inch shade	$3.65	Complete	$10.05	
" " "	" "	1 "	6.40	—	10 "	5.50 4.25	"	11.90 10.65	
" " C 3094	9 "	2 "	9.10	—	12 "	9.10 8.45	"	18.20 17.55	
" " "	" "	2 "	9.10	—	14 "	11.85 10.00	"	20.95 19.00	
" " C 3095	12 "	2 "	11.40	—	16 "	14.55 10.75	"	25.95 22.15	
" " "	" "	3 "	12.30	—	18 "	18.20 18.10	"	30.50 25.40	
" " C 3096	15 "	3 "	16.40	—	18 "	18.20 13.10	"	34.60 29.50	
" " "	" "	3 "	16.40	—	20 "	21.85 16.90	"	38.25 33.30	

THE PAIRPOINT CORPORATION, New Bedford, Mass.
SALES ROOMS:

New York	Chicago	Montreal	San Francisco
43 West 23rd St.	402 Columbus Bldg.	Coristine Bldg.	140 Geary St.

Plate 557. Copley shade. Sunset decoration #862. Base #C3093 (mahogany). 1915.

Base Solid Mahogany Brass Trimmed				Shade Copley Shape No. 863 Poinsetta Decoration		
Base No. C 3093 7 inch	1 Light	$6.40 —	8 inch shade	$3.65	Complete	$10.05
" " " " "	1 "	6.40 — 10	" "	5.50	"	11.90
" " C 3094 9 "	2 "	9.10 — 12	" "	8.20	"	17.30
" " " " "	2 "	9.10 — 14	" "	10.95	"	20.05
" " C 3095 12 "	2 "	11.40 — 16	" "	13.65	"	25.05
" " " " "	3 "	12.30 — 18	" "	16.40	"	28.70
" " C 3096 15 "	3 "	16.40 — 18	" "	16.40	"	32.80
" " " " "	3 "	16.40 — 20	" "	20.00	"	36.40

THE PAIRPOINT CORPORATION, New Bedford, Mass.
SALES ROOMS:

New York	Chicago	Montreal	San Francisco
43 West 23rd St.	402 Columbus Bldg.	Coristine Bldg.	140 Geary St.

Plate 558. Copley shade. Poinsettia decoration #863. Base #C3093 (mahogany). 1915.

Base Old Brass, Flemish Brass   **Shade Exeter Shape**
Bronze and New Antique Finish   **No. 551 Harvest Decoration**

Base No.	D 3040	7½ inch	1 Light	$6.85	8½ inch shade	$6.40	Complete	$13.25
" "	D 3041	12 "	2 "	15.45	15 " "	15.45	"	30.90
" "	D 3042	13¼ "	2 "	17.25	17½ " "	20.00	"	37.25
" "	"	"	3 "	18.65	17½ " "	20.00	"	38.65
" "	D 3043	15 "	3 "	20.90	20 " "	24.50	"	45.40

THE PAIRPOINT CORPORATION, New Bedford, Mass.

New York   Chicago   Montreal   San Francisco
43 West 23rd St.   402 Columbus Bldg.   Coristine Bldg.   140 Geary St.

Plate 559. Exeter shade. Harvest decoration #551. Base #D3040. 1915.

Base Old Brass, Flemish Brass
Bronze and New Antique Finish

Shade Exeter Shape
No. 553 English Landscape Decoration

Base No.											
	D 3040	7½ inch	1 Light	$6.85—	8½ inch shade	$6.40	Complete	$13.25
" "	D 3041	12 "	2 "	15.45—15	" "	15.45	"	30.90
" "	D 3042	13¼ "	2 "	17.25—17½	" "	20.00	"	37.25
" "		"	3 "	18.65—17½	" "	20.00	"	38.65
" "	D 3043	15 "	3 "	20.90—20	" "	24.50	"	45.40

THE PAIRPOINT CORPORATION, New Bedford, Mass.

New York	Chicago	Montreal	San Francisco
43 West 23rd St.	402 Columbus Bldg.	Coristine Bldg.	140 Geary St.

Plate 560. Exeter shade. English Landscape decoration #553. Base #D3040. 1915.

**Base Old Brass, Flemish Brass
Bronze and New Antique Finish**

**Shade Exeter Shape
No. 446 La Chinois Decoration**

Base No.	D 3040	7½ inch	1 Light	$6.85—	8½ inch shade	$6.25	Complete	$13.10
"	" D 3041	12 "	2 "	15.45—	15 " "	15.00	"	30.45
"	" "	12 "	3 "	16.85—	15 " "	15.00	"	31.85
"	" D 3042	13¼ "	2 "	17.25—	17½ " "	19.40	"	36.65
"	" "	13¼ "	3 "	18.65—	17½ " "	19.40	"	38.05
"	" D 3043	15 "	3 "	20.90—	20 " "	24.40	"	45.30

THE PAIRPOINT CORPORATION, New Bedford, Mass.

New York
43 West 23rd St.

San Francisco
140 Geary St.

Montreal
Coristine Bldg.

Plate 561 and 562. Exeter shade. La Chinois decoration #446. Base #D3040. 1915-1922.

Base Old Brass, Flemish Brass   **Shade Exeter Shape**
Bronze and New Antique Finish   **No. 554 Sèvres Decoration**

Base No.				Light			shade		Complete
D 3040	7½ inch	1	"	$6.85—	8½ inch	"	$6.40	"	$13.25
D 3041	12 "	2	"	15.45—15	"	"	15.45	"	30.90
D 3042	13¼ "	2	"	17.25—17½	"	"	20.00	"	37.25
"	"	3	"	18.65—17½	"	"	20.00	"	38.65
D 3043	15 "	3	"	20.90—20	"	"	23.65	"	44.55

THE PAIRPOINT CORPORATION, New Bedford, Mass.

New York	Chicago	Montreal	San Francisco
43 West 23rd St.	402 Columbus Bldg	Coristine Bldg.	140 Geary St.

Plate 563. Exeter shade. Sevres decoration #554. Base #D3040. 1915.

**Base Old Brass, Flemish Brass
Bronze and New Antique Finish**

**Shade Exeter Shape
No. 445 The Seasons Decoration**

Base No.	D 3048	7½ inch	1	Light	$6.85—	8½ inch shade	$6.35	Complete	$13.20
"	D 3049	12 "	2	"	14.10—15	" "	15.45	"	29.55
"	"	12 "	3	"	15.45—15	" "	15.45	"	30.90
"	D 3050	13½ "	2	"	15.45—17½	" "	20.00	"	35.45
"	"	13½ "	3	"	16.85—17½	" "	20.00	"	36.85
"	D 3051	15 "	3	"	19.10—20	" "	24.50	"	43.60

THE PAIRPOINT CORPORATION, New Bedford, Mass.

New York
43 West 23rd St.

San Francisco
140 Geary St.

Montreal
Coristine Bldg.

Plate 564. Exeter shade. The Seasons decoration #445. Base #D3048. 1915-1922.

Old Brass, Egyptian Brass, Flemish, Antique and Bronze Finish

Shade Exeter Shape No. 478
Decoration Persian

Base D3065	8 inch	1 Light	$6.00 — 8½ inch shade	$5.00	Complete	$11.00
Base D3066	12½ inch	2 Light	12.00 — 15 inch shade	16.00	Complete	28.00
Base D3066	12½ inch	3 Light	13.35 — 15 inch shade	16.00	Complete	29.35
Base D3067	14 inch	2 Light	14.00 — 17½ inch shade	20.00	Complete	34.00
Base D3067	14 inch	3 Light	15.35 — 17½ inch shade	20.00	Complete	35.35
Base D3068	15½ inch	3 Light	17.30 — 20 inch shade	24.00	Complete	41.30

THE PAIRPOINT CORPORATION, New Bedford, Mass.

New York
43 West 23d Street

San Francisco
Hammond Building, 278 Post Street

Montreal
Coristine Building

Plate 565. Exeter shade. Persian decoration #478. Base #D3065. 1924-1926.

Base Old Brass, Flemish Brass, Bronze and New Antique Finish					Shade Landsdowne Shape No. 314 New England Autumn Decoration			
Base No. D3056	7	inch	1 Light	$7.50 —	8½ inch shade	$5.00	Complete	$12.50
" " D3057	12	"	2 "	13.35 —	16 " "	13.35	"	26.70
" " "	"	"	3 "	14.65 —	16 " "	13.35	"	28.00
" " D3058	13	"	2 "	15.35 —	18 " "	16.00	"	31.35
" " "	"	"	3 "	16.65 —	18 " "	16.00	"	32.65
" " D3059	14	"	3 "	19.35 —	20 " "	20.00	"	39.35

THE PAIRPOINT CORPORATION, New Bedford, Mass.

New York:
43 West 23rd Street

San Francisco:
140 Geary Street

Montreal:
Coristine Bldg.

Plate 566. Lansdowne shade. New England Autumn decoration #314. Base #D3056. 1915-1922.

Base Old Brass, Flemish Brass, Bronze and New Antique Finish				Shade Landsdowne Shape No. 453 San Souci Decoration		
Base No. D3056 7 inch	1 Light	$7.50	8½ inch shade	$4.00	Complete	$11.50
" " D3057 12 "	2 "	13.35	16 "	10.65	"	24.00
" " " " "	3 "	14.65	16 "	10.65	"	25.30
" " D3058 13 "	2 "	15.35	18 "	13.35	"	28.70
" " " " "	3 "	16.65	18 "	13.35	"	30.00
" " D3059 14 "	3 "	19.35	20 "	17.30	"	36.65

THE PAIRPOINT CORPORATION, New Bedford, Mass.

New York: 43 West 23rd St.   San Francisco: 140 Geary St.   Montreal: Coristine Bldg.

Plate 567. Lansdowne shade. San Souci decoration #453. Base #D3056. 1924-1926.

Old Brass, Egyptian Brass, Flemish, Antique and Bronze Finish

Shade Lansdowne Shape No. 476 Decoration Persian

Base D3065	8 inch	1 Light	$6.00 — 8½ inch shade $4.65	Complete $10.65
Base D3066	12½ inch	2 Light	12.00 — 16 inch shade 14.70	Complete 26.70
Base D3066	12½ inch	3 Light	13.35 — 16 inch shade 14.70	Complete 28.05
Base D3067	14 inch	2 Light	14.00 — 18 inch shade 18.00	Complete 32.00
Base D3067	14 inch	3 Light	15.35 — 18 inch shade 18.00	Complete 33.35
Base D3068	15½ inch	3 Light	17.30 — 20 inch shade 21.35	Complete 38.65

THE PAIRPOINT CORPORATION, New Bedford, Mass.

New York — 43 West 23d Street
San Francisco — Hammond Building, 278 Post Street
Montreal — Coristine Building

Plate 568. Lansdowne shade. Persian decoration #476. Base #D3065. 1924-1926.

		Base Solid Mahogany Brass Trimmed					Shade Touraine Shape No. 870 Brigs Decoration		
Base No.	C 3093	7 inch	1 Light	$6.40	— 8 inch shade	$5.00	Complete	$11.40	
"	" "	" "	1 "	6.40	— 10 " "	6.85	"	13.25	
"	C 3094	9 "	2 "	9.10	— 12 " "	8.65	"	17.75	
"	C 3095	12 "	2 "	11.40	— 14 " "	11.40	"	22.80	
"	" "	" "	2 "	11.40	— 16 " "	~~14.55~~ 12.75 "	"	~~25.95~~ 24.15	
"	" "	" "	3 "	12.30	— 16 " "	~~14.55~~ 12.75 "	"	~~26.85~~ 25.05	
"	C 3096	15 "	3 "	16.40	— 18 " "	~~18.20~~ 15.45	"	~~34.60~~ 31.85	

THE PAIRPOINT CORPORATION, New Bedford, Mass.
SALES ROOMS:

New York	Chicago	Montreal	San Francisco
43 West 23rd St.	402 Columbus Bldg.	Coristine Bldg.	140 Geary St.

Plate 569. Touraine shade. Brigs decoration #870. Base #C3093 (mahogany). 1915.

Plate 570. Touraine shade. Rookwood decoration #869. Base #C3093 (mahogany). 1915.

**Base Solid Mahogany
Brass Trimmed**

**Shade Touraine Shape
No. 873 Dresden Decoration**

Base No.									
C 3093	7 inch	1 Light	$6.40	—	8 inch shade	$6.40	Complete	$12.80
"	"	"	"	1 "	6.40	— 10 "	"	7.75	"	14.15
"	C 3094	9 "	2 "	9.10	— 12 "	"	10.00	"	19.10
"	C 3095	12 "	2 "	11.40	— 14 "	"	11.85	"	23.25
"	"	"	2 "	11.40	— 16 "	"	14.55	"	25.95
"	"	"	3 "	12.30	— 16 "	"	14.55	"	26.85
"	C 3096	15 "	3 "	16.40	— 18 "	"	20.00	"	36.40

THE PAIRPOINT CORPORATION, New Bedford, Mass.
SALES ROOMS:

New York	Chicago	Montreal	San Francisco
43 West 23rd St.	402 Columbus Bldg.	Coristine Bldg.	140 Geary St.

Plate 571. Touraine shade. Dresden decoration #873. Base #C3093 (mahogny). 1915.

Base Solid Mahogany Brass Trimmed					Shade Touraine Shape No. 872 Decoration (Green Leather effect)			
Base No. C 3093	7 inch	1 Light	$6.40 —	8 inch shade	$4.55	Complete	$10.95
" " "	7 "	1 "	6.40 —	10 " "	6.40	"	12.80
" " C 3094	9 "	2 "	9.10 —	12 " "	8.20	"	17.30
" " C 3095	12 "	2 "	11.40 —	14 " "	10.00	"	21.40
" " "	" "	2 "	11.40 —	16 " "	12.75	"	24.15
" " "	" "	3 "	12.30 —	16 " "	12.75	"	25.05
" " C 3096	15 "	3 "	16.40 —	18 " "	15.90	"	32.30

THE PAIRPOINT CORPORATION, New Bedford, Mass.
SALES ROOMS:

New York	Chicago	Montreal	San Francisco
43 West 23rd St.	402 Columbus Bldg.	Coristine Bldg.	140 Geary St.

Plate 572. Touraine shade. Green Leather decoration #872. Base # C3093 (mahogany). 1915.

The Pairpoint lamp catalog continues with Plates #1 through #288 in another volume, *Pairpoint Lamp Catalog, Shade Shapes Ambero through Panel.*

Index

The Index refers to the Plate numbers, not pages.
The Plates are found in two volumes: Plates 1 through 288 are in *Pairpoint Lamp Catalog, Shade Shapes Ambero through Panel* and Plates 289 through 572 are in *Pairpoint Lamp Catalog, Shade Shapes Papillon through Windsor & Related Materials*.

Ambero shade, 1-3, 82, 527, 556

Balmoral shade, 513, 514
Baltimore shade, 4-8
Begonia shade, 9
Berkley shade, 10-17, 531, 533, 534, 537
Berlin shade, 18-21
Bethoven shade, 22
Blenheim shade, 23, 24
Bombay shade, 25, 532-539, 543-546
Boston shade, 26-32
Boudoir Lamps, 529, 530
Bridge (parchment) shade, 146-148
Bristol shade, 33-36, 325

Cambridge shade, 37-40
Camden shade, 41
Candles shade, 42, 43
Capri shade, 44-50, 257
Carlisle shade, 51-64, 531, 534, 538, 539, 547-552
Carmela shade, 65, 342
Carmelia shade, 341
Chesterfield shade, 66-71
Chestnut shade, 72
Cologne shade, 73-75
Colona shade, 76-81
Colonial shade, 82, 529, 530
Concord shade, 150
Cone shade, 83, 84
Copley shade, 85-87, 525-527, 553-558
Cremona shade, 65, 88-89, 341
Crystal shade (Astral lamp), 90

Dartmouth shade, 91
Devonshire shade, 92-94
Directoire shade, 95-109

Easter Lily shade, 454
Electric urn, 458-463
Empire Parchment shade, 110-113, 520-524
Exeter shade, 114-116, 540, 559-562, 563-565

Floral shade, 117-124
Florence shade, 125-134

Genoa shade, 135-142
Globe shade, 143
Grape shade, 144, 145

Junior (parchment) shade, 146-148

Lansdowne shade, 149, 531, 534, 541, 566-568
Lexington shade, 150
Lilac shade, 151-156, 258
Lily shade, 157
Livorno shade, 158-164
Lotus shade, 50, 165, 166, 349
Lucca shade, 167-173

Magenta shade, 174-185
Malta shade, 186-194
Manchester shade, 195
Marlborough shade, 196-200
Melon shade, 201-206
Milano shade, 207-210

287

Modena shade, 211
Mozart shade, 212, 213
Murano shade, 214-237

Napoli shade, 238, 239
Nausett shade, 240
Naushon shade, 241
Newport shade, 44, 150
Night Lamps, 529, 530
Normandie shade, 242-244

Oval Shield shade (parchment), 519
Oxford shade, 245-249

Palm shade, 154, 256-268
Palmero shade, 250-255
Panel shade, 269-288
Papillon shade, 289-294, 529, 530
Paris shade, 295
Pisa shade, 296-298
Plymouth shade, 299-317
Poinsettia shade, 318
Pompey shade, 319-324
Pond lily shade, 33, 325, 348
Poppy shade, 326-328
Portsmouth shade, 329-337, 453

Ravenna shade, 338-340
Resina shade, 341-342

Roma shade, 343, 344
Rose shade, 259, 345-352, 409

San Reno shade, 353, 354
Savoy shade, 355, 356
Seville shade, 360-379
Shield shade (parchment), 515-517, 519
Sorento shade, 357-359
Springfield shade, 34, 195, 380-403
Square shade (parchment), 518
Stratford shade, 345, 404-412, 532

Tisbury shade (Astral lamp), 413
Tivoli shade, 414-434
Torino shade, 435-437
Touraine shade, 438-450, 528, 533, 542, 569-572
Tulip shade, 451-454
Tuscanna shade, 455-457

Venice shade, 464-468
Vienna shade, 469-508
Violet Bouquet shade, 256

Wagner shade, 509, 510
Wakefield shade, 511, 512
Warwick shade, 513, 514
Windsor shade, 513, 514
Worwick, see Warwick